David Lav

July '91

1995

The Medieval Warhorse

THAMES AND HUDSON

The Medieval Warhorse

Origin, Development and Redevelopment

R.H.C. DAVIS

with
50 illustrations

For Eleanor
without whose
encouragement and support
this book would not
have been written

Contents

Introduction

Many of my friends have expressed surprise that I should have embarked on a history of horsebreeding. In fact my interest in the subject has arisen directly from the early history of Normandy. When writing a book entitled *The Normans and their Myth*, I could not help reflecting on the ease with which the Normans recruited foreigners. When I asked what the attraction for these foreigners was, I could only conclude that it was the lure of joining an outstandingly successful army, whose power was founded on the very large number of warhorses at its disposal. How had the Normans obtained these horses?

It was not an easy question to answer, for though historians had long realized the necessity of studying the development of a knight's armour, hardly anyone had given any attention to the horse. The assumption seems to have been that horses of the right type were provided by Nature in unlimited quantities. That simply was not true. In North-West Europe, where mounted knights were to be found earlier and in greater numbers than in any other part of the medieval world, the indigenous horse was no larger than a Shetland pony. By the eleventh century, if not before, someone had somehow discovered how to produce large numbers of horses which were bigger.

In many ways this discovery shaped the society of the Middle Ages, for that society depended on horses more than any other before or since. The fact is reflected in two key words which are amongst the first to be used whenever the Middle Ages are mentioned, feudalism and chivalry. 'Chivalry' is derived from *cheval*, the French word for a horse, and originally meant horsemanship. Knights – *chevaliers* – were horsemen because they were by definition mounted warriors who fought on horseback.

The society which maintained them was called 'feudal', because land tenure was based on fiefs (medieval Latin *feodum, feudum*) or estates held by knights in return for military service, and for that service horses were indispensable.

It was for this reason that in 1943 the American medievalist Carl Stephenson declared that the origin of feudalism would be 'found by studying the introduction of the thoroughbred charger or destrier whose size and strength permitted the mailed warrior to fight on horseback'. He added that he had 'no positive evidence to offer' himself, but he clearly hoped that his spirited exposition would inspire a younger historian to investigate the matter. I know that at the time I felt that this was a challenge which could not be ignored, because I made a very careful note of his words. But having done so, I forgot about them, or rather tucked them away into the inner recesses of my mind where they remained dormant until some thirty years later a fresh experience awakened them.

The experience was a visit to 'The Genius of China' at the Royal Academy in London during the winter of 1973–4. The centrepiece of that exhibition was a bronze 'flying horse' poised with one leg on a swallow's back. It had been excavated at Wu-Wei in Kansu in 1969. The catalogue and pictorial displays explained that this figure represented one of the 'celestial' horses descended from those captured by the Chinese in Ferghana and Sogdiana in 101 BC and as such depicted the ancestral type of all horses as we know them today. For the West-Central Asian horses had been discovered also by the peoples of the Middle and Near East, notably the Hittites and the Persians, through whom they reached the Arabs who (as the exhibition demonstrated on enormous maps) had taken them with their armies along the African coast of the Mediterranean and into Spain. When I visited the exhibition I was already working on the Normans, and already puzzled about their horses. I knew that some Normans had taken part in the reconquest of Spain, and consequently I remembered Carl Stephenson's words.

It was a great stroke of luck that at almost the same time, when browsing in a bookshop, I saw a book by Miklós Jankovich, *They Rode into Europe* (London, 1971). No doubt I should have seen it

16

7

sooner, because it had been published two years before, but I bought it at once. It was one of the most timely purchases I have ever made. The book fired my imagination and convinced me that the study of horsebreeding could open up new historical vistas. It also warned me against thinking of 'the introduction of the thoroughbred charger' (Carl Stephenson's words) as if it was the launching of a new car which, once designed, could be manufactured to a uniform pattern. Jankovich made me realize that the establishment of a breed was a very slow business, extending over scores of years if not centuries; that even when established it was impossible for a breed to remain absolutely permanent; and that any breed which was not carefully guarded could be 'lost' far more quickly than it could ever be re-established.

I have explained my approach to medieval horsebreeding because it is important for the reader to understand that any new contribution which I can make in this book will not be zoological or equestrian but historical. I shall start with a sketch of the development of cavalry warfare in the Middle Ages in order to show what sort of horses were required. I shall then consider the methods by which selective breeding could have been attempted in a pre-scientific age, and then turn to the evidence for the ways in which those methods were applied to the development of the warhorse, both in Europe generally and in England. Finally I shall endeavour to show how and why it was that breeders abandoned the idea of producing 'great' horses and developed a new type which in England became known as the English Thoroughbred.

Naturally I have had more opportunity for research in England than in Europe, and consequently the chapters on England are more detailed. I cannot pretend to have resolved all the difficulties which I have encountered, but I have endeavoured not to smooth them over, hoping that subsequent scholars will be able to pick up some useful clues from those facts which I have found baffling. A particular difficulty has been vocabulary, because the terms used to denote different breeds, types or even colours of horse change bewilderingly from century to century and from country to country (see the Glossary, pp. 135–8). As an example of these difficulties I have attempted, in Appendix I, a literal translation of Jordanus Ruffus's thirteenth-century account of how to judge the points of a horse (p. 132). The basic difficulty is that until the end of the Middle Ages, few people who actually worked with horses – shoeing them, grooming them, nursing them or selling them – were literate. They had learned their trade by working under older men who spoke in the vernacular, adding odd words which they had learned from foreign colleagues or upper-class employers. Old-fashioned words were current in some stables longer than in others, and French, German, English, Italian or Spanish words were mispronounced and transformed by farriers of different nationalities, before being latinized by a clerk whose interest was limited to the finances involved, or a learned 'vet' who assumed that everyone knew what he was talking about.

Throughout this work I have been helped by many friends and colleagues in Birmingham, Oxford, and at the Huntington Library at San Marino, California. At Birmingham I owe a very special debt to Dr C. C. Dyer and Dr John Langdon, at Oxford to Mr James Campbell, and in the USA to Professor Bernard Bachrach. Mr G. J. R. Hovell, Supervisor of Veterinary Studies in the University of Oxford, gave valuable help with the translation of Jordanus in Appendix I, and Professor Daniel I. Rubinstein of Princeton University has read the typescript and given me much help on wild horses and breeding. On particular points I have also received help from Dr Daniel Waley, Keeper of the Department of Manuscripts of the British Library, Professor Michael Swanton of the University of Exeter, Miss M. J. O. Kennedy of Edinburgh, Dr Margaret Wade Labarge of Ottawa, and Mr J. M. Wilkinson of the Waverton Stud at Sezincote, Gloucestershire. Finally, my editor at Thames and Hudson has been exceptionally helpful and meticulous in her oversight of the text. To these and countless others I offer my warmest thanks.

2 *A knight of the Palais family of Toulouse, depicted on his sarcophagus, c.1292. The knight's shield and the horse's housing (the caparison or covering of leather or cloth) display his coat of arms.*

1
Medieval Cavalry Warfare

Cavalry was the essential feature of a medieval army, and the knights who formed it were the essential feature of medieval society. But no one could be a knight unless he had a horse, and the horse had to be of the right quality. It had to be strong enough to carry an armed knight at a gallop, tall enough to dominate the opposing infantry, steady enough not to panic at the sound of battle, brave enough to bear wounds, and fierce enough to take an aggressive part in the fight, without losing the advantage of its natural agility. Such horses were not easy to find, and certainly they did not occur naturally. Consequently the business of acquiring and producing warhorses was a major industry in the Middle Ages, comparable to the breeding of racehorses in our own day. Ideally the breeders and dealers had to try to anticipate military developments, so that with every change of armour or tactics they could produce horses suitable for the new requirements, but few of them can have succeeded. Most probably they were always trying to catch up with the last development but one, for the techniques of war kept on changing.

To some extent cavalry had always been used, both in the Roman Empire and in the barbarian kingdoms;[1] but the numbers do not seem to have been large until the eighth century when the demand for cavalry increased dramatically. The German historian Heinrich Brunner associated this demand with the need to defend the Frankish kingdom from the Moslems of Spain. He attached great importance to Charles Martel's victory over them at Poitiers in 732, and observed that from the middle of the eighth century the Frankish kings were endowing their warriors with lands taken from the Church, so that they could have the resources necessary to equip and train themselves as an effective cavalry. The warriors became the king's vassals and received their lands as 'benefices' which were in theory revocable if the correct military service was not performed. This development is usually regarded as the beginning of feudalism, the word being due to the fact that benefices were eventually known as 'fiefs' (Latin *feoda, feuda*).

Whether Brunner was right or not in thus associating the battle of Poitiers with the origins of feudalism, there can be no doubt that in the eighth and ninth centuries both the number of benefices and the number of mounted soldiers grew very much larger. Estimates of precise numbers have varied widely, but the most recent, those of K. F. Werner, suggest that in the early years of the ninth century Charlemagne was entitled to the service of about 36,000 horsemen, drawn from all parts of his empire,[2] most of them supplied by counts and vassals who had been endowed with benefices specifically for their support. In a summons to the Abbot of St Quentin, Charlemagne stipulated that every horseman (*caballarius*) should have 'a shield, lance, long-sword, short-sword, bow, quiver and arrows.'[3] Ernoul le Noir in a panegyric on Louis the Pious, written *c.* 826–8, boasted of the size of the horses bred on Frankish soil, and alleged that their great height made them difficult to mount, but contemporary illustrations do not bear him out.[4] A drawing in the Sacramentary of Gellone, which is thought to date from *c.* 790–95, makes the horseman look bulkier than his horse, and a later drawing from the St Gallen Psalter (*c.* 890–924) makes it very clear that the horses are lightly built and relatively small.

In recent years Professor Bernard S. Bachrach has challenged the importance of the cavalry in Charlemagne's army.[5] He does not deny its existence or the obvious efforts made to maintain and improve it, but he reduces its practical use to 'search-and-destroy missions against small groups of relatively untrained enemies' and a supporting role in siege warfare and garrison duties; when it came to major battles the horsemen were, in his opinion, most likely to dismount and fight on foot. It is true that that was what happened at the battle of the Dyle in 891, but the Annals of Fulda expressly tell

23

3

3 *Carolingian cavalry, armed with lances and a bow and wearing chain-mail armour, attack a fortified town. Note the stirrups and the low saddles. From the St Gallen Psalter, c. 890–924.*

us how risky this was 'because the Franks were not used to fighting on foot'.[6] Professor Bachrach relies on the account of the battle of the Süntel in 782, in which a body of Frankish horsemen were defeated by the Saxons, at whom they had ridden as fast as their horses would carry them, as if they were pursuing fugitives from behind. But the criticism of the annalist is not that these Franks fought on horseback, but that they did not wait for the main part of their army, being so anxious to win the victory before it arrived that they had advanced in complete disarray. No charge is effective if everyone is attempting to go as fast as he can without regard to the pace of his fellows.[7]

That cavalry was expected to ride at the enemy is shown by the many stories of infantry defending themselves by digging trenches in front of their position, and concealing them with brushwood so that the enemy's cavalry would fall into them. In Britain the most famous employment of this ruse was by the Scots at the battle of Bannockburn (1314), but the general principle of the stratagem was known at least as early as the sixth century. Gregory of Tours, who died in 593, alleged that the Thuringians tried it out on King Theuderic (d. 534):

> They dug ditches in the future field of battle, and covered them over closely with sods, so that they seemed part of the unbroken plain. When the encounter began, numbers of Frankish horsemen fell into these ditches and were sorely hindered; though when the trick was once discovered, they began to look more cautiously about them.[8]

On this occasion the Franks were able to recover from the initial setback and win the victory, an eventuality which would have been impossible if they had been charging as in the fourteenth century. Their advance on horseback cannot have been in a solid phalanx with one rank behind another. It must have been accomplished in some other way.

What this was is suggested by the abridgement of a fourth-century military handbook, Vegetius's *De Re Militari*, which was made c. 856 by Rabanus Maurus for King Lothair II. Rabanus stated that in the abridgement he would retain only those items which could still be useful in his own day. Amongst these was Vegetius's description of how men should be taught to mount and dismount.

> Wooden horses are placed during the winter under a roof, and in summer in a field. The recruits at first try to mount unarmed, then they mount carrying shields and swords, and finally with very large pole weapons. And this practice was so thorough that they were forced to learn how to jump on and off their horses not only from the right but from the left and from the rear, and in addition they learnt to jump on and off their horses even with an unsheathed sword.

'Indeed,' added Rabanus, 'the exercise of jumping [on and off one's horse] has flourished greatly among the Frankish people.'[9]

This jumping or leaping on and off the horse has to be borne in mind in all discussions of Frankish tactics, and particularly when it comes to the question of the use of the lance. Military historians have pointed out that in principle it can be used in four different ways: (1) hurled like a javelin, (2) thrust downwards as in pig-sticking, (3) thrust upwards so as to lift an opponent off his horse, or (4) held 'couched' (French *couché*) while one charged one's opponent at speed. Generally speaking it is believed that this last method, which eventually became the norm, was not significantly used until the twelfth century, but the uncertainties of the matter are well illustrated by the account of an individual attack (allegedly in 578) which is given by Gregory of Tours:

> [Dragolen] struck spurs to his horse and charged Guntram at full speed. But his blow failed, for his spear [*astili*] broke, and his sword fell to the ground. Guntram . . . then, raising his lance [*contu*] struck Dragolen in the throat and unseated him. And as Dragolen was hanging from his horse, one of Guntram's friends thrust a lance [*lancia*] into his side and gave him the finishing blow.[10]

At first sight it might look as if Dragolen was charging Guntram with his lance couched, but if so it would be hard to explain why his sword fell to the ground. It seems more likely that Dragolen hurled his spear (method 1) and then galloped at Guntram to strike him with his sword; and since Guntram raised his lance in order to strike Dragolen in the throat and unseat him, it looks as if he must first have jumped off his horse.

Such jumping would have become far more difficult when the front and back of the saddle were raised to form a pommel and cantle. This development of the saddle, first attested in the Bayeux Tapestry, shows that by the second half of the eleventh century the emphasis had changed from rapid jumping on and off one's horse to keeping a firm seat while heavy blows were delivered. The tapestry shows that those blows could be delivered in a number of different ways. It depicts an opening charge led by a knight with his spear in the couched position, but on close inspection we find that

6

4 there is only one other Norman with lance couched, as opposed to
sixteen who are hurling their lances (some of them in the opening
5 charge), seven thrusting them downwards, five upwards, and
(particularly towards the end of the sequence) seven who have
abandoned their lances in favour of swords. In this latter case a
knight might raise himself upright on his stirrups and strike
downward, but if he lost his balance he might fall in front of the
pommel of his saddle and be unable to regain his seat.

It will be noticed also that a great deal of use is now being made
of the stirrups. The knights with couched lances lean forward,
pressing hard on their stirrups; those who are hurling their lances
are almost standing on their stirrups. The shields also have changed
from Carolingian times. They are no longer circular but kite-
shaped, the additional length being used to protect not so much the
knight's exposed left leg as his horse's back, the point of the shield
nearly always trailing behind the knight. Whatever its advantage
on horseback its size would have been a serious disadvantage in

4, 5 *(opposite and above) Two details from the Bayeux Tapestry, showing Norman knights charging the English. In the first section, the front three are about to hurl their lances, while the fourth has his couched. In the second, the four leading knights are 'pig-sticking' with their lances; the fifth wields his sword.*

6 *(right) The Conqueror's horse is led up to him before the battle. The saddle has a pommel and cantle, and the stallion displays his masculinity. From the Bayeux Tapestry.*

EXIERVNT:DEHESTENGA:

fighting on foot, since unlike the circular shield it could not be used as an offensive weapon (cf. p. 60).[11]

The Bayeux Tapestry is also explicit that the warhorses were stallions. This was the case throughout the Middle Ages. The warhorse was expected to fight in the battle himself, kicking, leaping and rearing at his opponents; he was encouraged to be ferocious, and for this reason was provided with a bit which was cruelly harsh on the mouth. Mares were not used in warfare in medieval Europe. All the good mares were kept fully occupied in the studs, and the others were considered suitable only for women or priests. Orderic Vitalis has a splendid story about William Rufus who, when he had to cross the Channel in a hurry in order to put down a rebellion, was prepared to make a fool of himself by riding a mare which he had borrowed from a priest.[12] But not even he would have dared to ride her into battle. Nor would he or anyone else in Western (as opposed to Eastern) Europe have fought on a gelding before the end of the Middle Ages, because it was then the belief, however unwarranted, that geldings lacked both dignity and courage (see the Glossary, pp. 135–6).

Finally, though the Bayeux Tapestry was evidently designed to glorify the Norman knights, it does give a hint that others played a part in the victory. The initial charge is supported by four bowmen on foot, and towards the end of the battle there are twenty-three Norman bowmen tucked away in the lower margin. Though their intervention does not count as a major incident in the narrative, it could well have been decisive. Well-directed arrows could penetrate chain mail, a fact which was to lead to a demand for plate armour to protect both the knight and the head and shoulders of his horse.

One of the problems facing military historians is to know the extent to which chronicles, epic poems or pictures depict what was actually there to be seen, or merely what was expected. It was an age of chivalric (or 'horsy') society, and everyone believed that battles could not possibly be won except by cavalry. One of the favourite books of the age, from the time of its composition, c. 1100, was the *Song of Roland*, whose most graphic passages describe the battle at Roncesvalles as a series of exploits by individual knights:

> The count Gerin astride his horse Sorel,
> And his companion Gerer on Passecerf
> Let go their reins and eagerly both spur
> And strike a Saracen named Timozel,
> One on the hauberk, the other on the shield.
> They break their lances off within his body
> And lay him dead among the fallow field.[13]

It would have been natural for twelfth-century knights to imagine themselves in similar roles and to be disappointed, if not incredulous, if the reality proved less heroic.

Fighting on horseback was their business, and they would have learnt to ride from infancy. At about the age of eight they would be sent to serve in the household of a more powerful lord. There, in addition to minding the lord's horses and armour, they would learn the basic skills, such as leaping into the saddle fully armed without touching the stirrup, and charging at a target with lance couched. The target, known as a quintain, was fixed on a cross-bar designed to swing round when hit. At one end of it was the target itself, at the other a sack of sand, so arranged that anyone who allowed himself to be halted by the impact of hitting the target would be knocked off his horse by the sandbag. The purpose of a charge was not just to hit one's opponent but to gallop through the enemy ranks so as to make them panic and flee.

From the knight's point of view the technique required great skill.[14] If one was to hold a lance horizontal and steady while galloping a horse, it was essential to secure the lance at more than a single point. If it was well balanced, one could hold it in one hand and tuck the rear end under one's armpit, but even this position was hard on the wrist, and could not be maintained for long. It was therefore normal for knights to hold their lance upright, not only when on the march, but also at the start of a charge,[15] resting it (from the middle of the twelfth to the fourteenth century) on a 'fewter' or felt butt on the saddle bow. As the charge developed,

19

and at the very last moment, the lances were lifted off the fewters and their points lowered or 'couched'. So as to ensure that the weight of the lance and the force of its blow did not unbalance the rider by being on his right side only, the point of the lance was held to the left of the horse's head with the base secured tightly under the rider's right armpit. Aim was taken by steering the horse and, if necessary, by twisting one's whole body in the saddle. If one hit one's target, the lance could easily break or be whipped out of one's grasp by the force of the blow. 7

These latter possibilities became increasingly likely as the armour of both man and horse became more effective. In the *Armor* Bayeux Tapestry the knights wear hauberks or coats of chain mail, which would have weighed about 25 lb (11 kg), only their helmets being of plate metal, while their horses have no armour at all. As has already been mentioned, they were vulnerable to archers. Consequently it became common for men to protect their breast with a small *plastron de fer* underneath the hauberk, and for horses to be protected with armour also. After a victory over the French in 1198, King Richard I announced that he had captured 200 horses, 140 of them 'clad in iron' (*cooperti de ferro*).[16] The weight that the horses had to carry was increasing steadily, and horsebreeders found that the best market was always for larger and stronger horses.

Historians and hippologists often argue about 'the medieval warhorse' as if its conformation and size were constant throughout the Middle Ages. In fact they were not constant at all, but were being developed the whole time, the size of the best warhorses increasing almost beyond recognition between the eleventh and the fourteenth centuries. The phrase 'great horse' (*magnus equus* or *grant chival*), which first appeared towards the end of the thirteenth century, rapidly became a technical term for a really good warhorse in the fourteenth. By contrast, Richard son of Ascletin, a Norman in eleventh-century Italy, was said to have ridden a horse so small that his feet touched the ground. Many of the horses in the Bayeux Tapestry do not look very much larger than that. Similarly the seals of William the Conqueror, his half-brother Odo of 8

7 Battle scene, painted most probably at the abbey of Bury St Edmunds c. 1135, showing knights lifting their spears off their fewters (top left) and then charging with them couched (below).

8, 9 The seal of Odo of Bayeux (d. 1097; left) depicts him on a small, light horse, suggestive of a Barb. The seal of Edward III (1340–72; right) shows a 'great horse' complete with armour and housing.

8 Bayeux, and his son William Rufus also show horses which are slim, small and without armour. From then on the horses depicted on seals grow larger and larger till those of Edward I and Edward III

9 are powerful animals of quite a different type.

The maximum size seems to have been reached in the fourteenth

10 century. It was in that century also that the weight of weapons and armour at last came under control. In spite of the common belief that the complete suits of plate armour produced in the fifteenth and sixteenth centuries were the heaviest of the Middle Ages, this

11 *Two jousting knights. They hold their heavy lances couched, securing them in a notch in the top right-hand corner of their shields. The horses wear armour on their heads (shaffrons) and shoulders.*

was not the case. They weighed about 50–60 lb (22–27 kg), which was less than the combination of hauberk and plate worn about 1300, when in addition to the *plastron de fer* there were strips of plate to protect the shoulders, arms, knees and legs.

Weapons also grew heavier until the fourteenth century, particularly the lance. The earliest reference to a heavy lance is in the Baligant extension of the *Song of Roland*, perhaps from the second quarter of the twelfth century:

> The emir holds the lance he calls Maltét,
> Its shaft is heavy, large as any club,
> The iron tip alone a full mule's load.[17]

As time went on, the lance could weigh as much as 30 or 40 lb (13–18 kg), and when it was couched the strain on the knight's wrist must have been enormous. In consequence he would rest his lance on the top edge of his shield, in which (after *c.* 1340) was cut a   11

< 10 *A really heavy 'great horse' of the second half of the fourteenth century, seen in a North Italian relief. The knight is wearing full plate armour over mail, so that the weight the horse had to carry must have been enormous.*

circular indent to hold it secure. The greatest problem, however, was to ensure that at the moment of shock the kick of the lance could be absorbed by the knight's body. For this purpose the lance was provided with a leather stop, somewhat like the button of an oar. If this was positioned so as to rest in front of the shield, the impact would ram it into the indent and force the whole shield against the knight's breastplate. Alternatively (after the 1390s) the stop could be fitted near the base of the lance and placed in front of a metal fitting attached to the right-hand side of the knight's breastplate. In either case the object was to weld horse, knight and lance into a single missile which could be launched at the enemy. The horse required was emphatically a great horse, agility being less important than unstoppable power.

A mounted knight such as has been described was expensive to equip and expensive to maintain. The weight of his lance was such that he no longer cared to carry it, even upright, unless he was in battle. The high war-saddle introduced in the middle of the fourteenth century did not provide him with a fewter on which to rest it, and so he had it carried for him by a squire. About the middle of the thirteenth century a new technical term, the *lance garnie*, was used to denote the mounted knight together with all the equipment and assistants which he now required. His assistants would have been one squire and two mounted archers. It would have been the squire's job to help the knight into his armour before the battle; the armour was far too heavy and hot to be worn day in and day out, so normally it would have been kept in boxes or bags on a packhorse in the squire's care.

12

12 A wounded horse, with armour covering its mane and a high war-saddle of the type introduced in the mid fourteenth century. From Jean de Wavrin's Chronique d'Angleterre, *late fifteenth century.*

13 *Armoured knights charging. The bases of their lances are fixed to their breastplates. The knights are in the front rank of each army and behind them are their assistants with inferior helmets. Detail from the family tree of the Austrian house of Babenberg, painted in 1489–93, showing here the Margrave Leopold II.*

A horse for each of the archers, another for the squire, and a packhorse for the luggage made a total of four. But in addition the knight had to have two for himself, a palfrey to ride in the ordinary course of events, and a warhorse for the battle. Since it was imperative that the warhorse should not already be tired before a battle began, it was never ridden on journeys, but led by the squire. When the battle approached the knight had to change both his clothes and his horse. This was the order of the day as early as *c.* 1100, for it is described in the *Song of Roland*; and though the

25

description purports to be of the Moslem army, it merely shows what any poet would have expected of the armies of his day.

> The pagans don their Saracen coats of mail,
> Most of them made of triple-layered chain,
> They lace good helmets made at Saragoce,
> Gird on their swords of good steel from Vienne.
> They all have fine shields and Valencian spears;
> All crimson, blue and white their gonfalons.
> They leave the palfreys and the mules behind
> And, mounting chargers, ride in close array.[18]

The business of equipping a knight for battle was cumbersome, labour-intensive and very expensive. The incidentals were endless. With six or more horses required for every knight, no army could rely on finding sufficient forage by the way; it had to carry a certain amount of fodder with it, thus increasing still further the number of horses required.

Robert Bruce exploited this weakness in the armies of King Edward I by the use of 'mounted infantry', in which the men wore protective clothing of leather rather than iron, and the mounts were ponies, which were not required to take part in the battle but merely to transport the infantry to it. Such mounted infantry could harass an army of knights on the march, but escape without having to give battle. In 1296 Edward I followed suit, hiring 260 *hobelars* or soldiers on small *hobyn* or 'hobby' horses from Ireland. After the battle of Bannockburn (1314) they became a regular feature of the English armies until, in the 1330s, they were replaced by mounted archers who filled the same role even more effectively. Archers also rode small light horses which carried no protective armour but were described as 'uncovered' (*discooperti*).[19]

At first mounted infantry and mounted archers were not intended as a replacement for mounted knights, but simply as a supplement. There was no reduction in the total number of horses required; gradually, however, there was a reduction in the number of *great* horses which were strictly necessary. This made some economy possible, but the rulers of Europe did not all appreciate

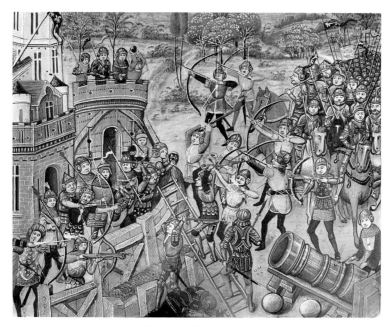

14 *Bowmen, crossbowmen, artillery and pikemen, with only a few great men on horses. From Jean de Wavrin's* Chronique d'Angleterre, *late fifteenth century.*

the possibility at once. The English reduced the numbers of their heavy cavalry in the middle of the fourteenth century, the French in the fifteenth, and the Italians only in the sixteenth.

The armoured knight was continually threatened by new weapons and new tactics. Cannon and handguns were becoming important in the fifteenth century, though their missiles were probably feared less than those of the improved crossbow made of steel and drawn by a windlass; its missiles could penetrate all but the very best armour. Most important of all, however, was the discovery of the effectiveness of well-trained infantry pikemen. Their first spectacular success was at the battle of Courtrai in 1302, where the French cavalry charged them without first reconnoitring the land, so that they discovered the existence of a canal across their route only when they were going too fast to stop. But even without the assistance of such egregious blunders, disciplined infantry could be more than a match for most cavalry. The chronicler Jehan de

15 Pikemen all-important. English troops on the march in Ireland led by the Lord Deputy, Sir Henry Sidney (father of Sir Philip), in 1576–8. The horsemen still wear armour, but it is now lighter.

Wavrin gave the following description of the pikemen in the army of Charles the Bold in 1471:

> Each had a sallet [helmet], jack [a doublet stuffed with tow], sword and pike, or long lance with a slender shaft and long sharp spear-head cutting on three sides. They were on foot and are called pikemen because they know better than anyone how to handle pikes . . . These pikes make very useful poles for placing a spike between two archers against the fearful effects of the cavalry trying to break their ranks, for there is no horse which, if struck in the chest with a pike, will not unfailingly die. These pikemen can also approach and attack cavalry from the side and pierce them right through, nor is there any armour, however good, that they cannot pierce or break.[20]

By the end of the sixteenth century there was little further use for knights fully encased in plate armour mounted on large and heavy horses; such cavalry as was required had to be light, with the men in far less elaborate armour and mounted on horses which were agile.

Nevertheless, old sentiments die hard. Some of the most splendid armour was made in the sixteenth century, some even in the seventeenth. The fact that in 1586 Sir Philip Sidney died of a bullet-wound in his left thigh caused one contemporary to mount a vigorous attack on those who 'scorne our auncient arming of our selues both on horseback and on foote, saying that wee armed ourselves in times past with too much armour (or peeces of iron as they terme it)'.[21] Jousting remained a noble sport and ensured the survival of many outdated accoutrements of war, including particularly the great medieval warhorse which, though no longer needed in large numbers, was still an object of esteem, still bred and still ridden. By the middle of the seventeenth century most people had realized that its real usefulness was finished, but in 1658 and 1667 William Cavendish (subsequently Duke of Newcastle) still thought it necessary to spell out its disadvantages:

> There are great disputes among cavaliers about this business: I will not trouble you much about their arguments but only deliver unto you my opinion. Those that are for high and large horses, say, they are strong for the shock. But they must know that all large horses are not strong; nay, for the most part they are not only the weakest horses, but commonly of no spirit or action.
>
> Put the case, a great horse were so strong, yet he is so tall and his strength diffused, and indeed so out of his strength, that a middling horse [entre deux selles], or rather a less horse, being under him and in his strength would certainly overthrow him. So that a middling horse or less is best for the war, or a single combat without doubt.[22]

The horse that had been good for heavy armour and heavy lance held rigid by its rider was no longer suitable for the battles of the English Civil War, and consequently the medieval warhorse was no longer produced. It had been the breeders' ideal for centuries, but in the 1650s and 1660s almost everyone at last recognized that it had become a thing of the past and that it would be more useful and profitable to produce a different type of horse.

16 A Chinese 'flying horse': bronze figure of the second century AD excavated at Wu-Wei, Kansu. The horse is supporting itself by one leg on a swallow, so as to emphasize the speed of the wonderful breed of 'celestial' or 'blood-sweating' horses which the Chinese had found in the area of Uzbekistan.

2

Origins and Methods of Horsebreeding

It was one thing for medieval cavalry commanders to know what sort of horses they wanted, quite another to find them. In North-West Europe, where the feudal cavalry first emerged, the indigenous horse was, as we have seen, uselessly small. If a horse more suitable for cavalry were to be found, it was essential to import livestock from abroad, and then to practise selective breeding on a very large scale.

The stock which was imported derived in part from Central Asia where, early in the first millennium BC, riding horses were bred in the region of the Altai Mountains. Excavations near Pazyryk have revealed remarkable burials with the bodies of horses deep-frozen in them. These horses have been divided into four different types, of which the finest, standing $14\frac{3}{4}$ or 15 hands high, was heavier than the modern Arabian but had features in common with it and could certainly have been used for cavalry.[1] Gradually they spread both east and west. The Chinese discovered them in 128 BC and were so impressed that twenty-seven years later they sent a military expedition to capture some. They succeeded in getting thirty which they took back to China, to form the foundation of a breed of 'celestial' or 'blood-sweating' horses which they immortalized in art.[2] The Chinese were not the first to discover these horses: they had already been taken westwards more than five hundred years earlier. Often known as Bactrian horses (Bactria being the modern Uzbekistan), their relatively large size made it possible for the armies of Western Asia to change over from chariot to cavalry warfare. The transition can be seen in the Assyrian reliefs from the Palace of Nineveh (c. 639 BC).

It was in the seventh century also that the Greeks acquired riding horses from Cyrene on the Mediterranean coast of Libya.

17 Horse and groom from Xanthos in Lycia (South-West Turkey), c. 470 BC. If the groom is to scale, the horse must be standing between fourteen and fifteen hands. A carpet or blanket is used as a saddle.

18 Horsemen from the frieze of the Parthenon at Athens, c. 447–432 BC. They are riding bareback.

Hippologists argue at length as to whether these horses had originated from Asia, or whether they had a separate origin,[3] but however that may be, it is certain that horse-riding was introduced into the Olympic games in 648 BC. By the fifth century BC the Greeks had also acquired large or 'sacred' horses which (according to Herodotus) were bred on the plains of Nisaea (now Nishapur in Iran). Carvings of these large horses have been found at Xanthos   17 and on the Mausoleum at Halikarnassos in the south-west corner of Asia Minor. Lighter types of horses used by the Greeks can be seen for example on the frieze of the Parthenon and on Syracusan coins.   18 All the main strains necessary for scientific breeding were thus available in the Eastern Mediterranean lands. In the fourth century BC Philip of Macedon and his son Alexander the Great were renowned for their cavalry. Alexander's own horse, Bucephalus, which died in India at the age of thirty, was almost certainly of Bactrian descent.

The Romans organized horsebreeding on a large scale, both for chariot racing and for cavalry, a fine example of one of their heavy chargers being depicted in the equestrian statue of Marcus Aurelius   19

19 Equestrian statue of Marcus Aurelius (AD 161–180) in Rome. In the Middle Ages it was thought to represent the Emperor Constantine, and small-scale copies of it occur on several Romanesque churches in France. It must have kept alive the idea of what a 'real' horse should look like.

(AD 161–180). The Roman studs were often located in places which were to remain famous for horsebreeding in medieval and modern times – in Asia Minor at the 'Villa Palmatii' (near Tyana in Cappadocia), in Spain, in Sicily, and on the karst lands of Apulia and Calabria in South Italy and Istria in north-west Yugoslavia, where the famous Lipizzaners were to be bred from the late sixteenth century onwards.[4] North Africa was particularly noted for racehorses, which the Romans called Numidian, and we would describe as 'Barbs' (i.e. from the Berber or 'Barbary' coast of North Africa). They ran in chariot races, and are illustrated in several mosaics, those of North Africa being noted for the number of horses which are named; we find, for instance, 'Amandus' (Lovely), 'Frumitas' (Delicious), 'Adorandus' (Adorable), and 'Crinitus' (Curly). Excavations made in the nineteenth century at the Baths of Pompeianus at Oued Athménia near Constantine in Algeria revealed both the remains of stables of exceptional size and mosaics depicting the stud farm with the horses' names over their individual stalls.

Because the main breeds of horse had all reached the Mediterranean countries by the time of the Roman Empire, it should not be thought that the supply of horses was assured for ever. On the contrary, it is a notorious fact that breeds can be 'lost' much more quickly than they can be established. Breeds are maintained by ensuring that good mares are not covered by any stallion which has not been specially selected. This means that, since male animals are extremely persistent in nosing out females in season, the mares have to be closely guarded. If they mated at will, the result would be disastrous. As Miklós Jankovich has put it:

It is notorious that feral horses – the descendants of runaway domestic horses – after only a few generations lose the properties conferred by domestication and resume more and more those of their wild ancestors. Thus the mustang of the American plains, now itself on the road to extinction, lost no time in shedding the attributes of the pure-bred Andalusian, and acquired recognizably those of several different ancestral

*20 A floor mosaic for a Roman horse-breeder at Hadrumetum (Sousse in Tunisia).
The tethered horses are named 'Amor', 'Dominator', 'Adorandus' and 'Crinitus'.*

21 *The horse of the future. Tenth-century drawing of an Arab horseman.*

الفرس بالماء

wild types. We may assume that its ancestors in the Old World had included Andalusian, Barb and the *Asturión* or pacing pony of Northern Iberia. All three in their turn were of composite wild ancestry. As these types once again began to 'separate out' in the process of wild breeding, natural selection again came into play, and 'survival factors' were the only forces that determined the ultimate constitution of mustang herds.[5]

An essential condition of successful horsebreeding is that there should be sufficient means to keep all good quality mares in captivity and to separate them from the males, either in stables or in a park surrounded by stallion-proof palings. In ordinary times this will prove expensive, but in time of civil disturbance or foreign invasion it is likely to be impossible. Fences will be broken down, mares will escape or be stolen, and be covered by every chance stallion they encounter. This is almost certainly what happened in the fourth, fifth and sixth centuries A D, when the Roman Empire in the West was collapsing under the pressure of the barbarian invasions. It was not that horses suddenly ceased to exist, but that the number of good quality horses declined dramatically, so that it became increasingly difficult to find sufficient mounts for a large force of cavalry.

That is why the Arabian horse became so important. The Arabs conquered Egypt, the whole North African coastline and Spain in the seventh and eighth centuries, and were halted only by the Franks under Charles Martel at the battle of Poitiers (732). The Arabs certainly fought on horseback, and though they may well have remounted much of their army in North Africa, which as we have seen was noted for fine horses in Roman times, they must have brought some of their own horses with them. These creatures were not indigenous to Arabia, where there do not seem to have been any horses much before the first century A D, the first to be acquired being almost certainly of Asiatic stock. But the Arabs made them very much their own because of the care they took over breeding.[6] In the desert, grass and fodder were in short supply, with the result that the number of horses that could be kept was strictly limited. It was therefore common sense to keep only the best, and since one stallion was sufficient to service many mares, surplus stallions were disposed of. It followed that the Arabian cavalry horse was (unlike the medieval warhorse of the West) almost always a mare and – most important for horsebreeding – that there were no undesirable stallions within reach of her. It was this fact that made it relatively easy in the desert to preserve the breed and ensure that it did not get lost.

The aim of a good horsebreeder is not just to maintain a breed but to improve it. According to the fashion of the day he may want a horse which is tall, medium or small, heavy or light, fierce or gentle, fast over short distances or long, and perhaps of some

21

specific colour. The breeder will seek out mares with as many as possible of the qualities required, and have them covered by a stallion who can complement them. Sometimes the resultant foals may reproduce the less desirable features of both their parents, but with luck one or two may combine the best of both. It is on them that the breeder will concentrate, ensuring that they mate only with other horses possessing the required qualities. At first this may well necessitate breeding 'in and in' ('there is no incest in horses', wrote William Cavendish) but subsequently the great art will be to introduce the right amount of new blood. To quote Cavendish again:

> I must tell you, that you must Never have a *Stallion* of your own *Breed*, because they are too far removed from the *Purity* and *Head* of the *Fountain*, which is a Pure *Spanish Horse*: Besides, should the *Stallions* be of your own Breed, in Three or Four *Generations* they would come to be *Cart-Horses*; so Gross and ill-Favoured would they be.[7]

How had the necessary arts and skills been developed? So far as can be seen there were three distinct stages in horsebreeding. In *Stage 1* there was a herd in which one stallion ran free with a number of mares and their colts, almost in a wild state. A clear account of it is found in Radloff's description of Kazakh and Kirghiz horsebreeding, as he saw it in Central Asia in the middle of the nineteenth century.

> A herd amounts most often to fifty animals, of which nine or ten are mares, each with a foal less than a year old, the rest being their yearling and older followers. The stallion as leader keeps the herd together, and also stands sentry over it. He has no fear of wolves, and it is only rarely that they manage to snatch a foal from him. And it must be a bold wolf at that. The stallion is ready to fight not only predators, but also rivals. The arrival of a strange stallion is a signal for a fight to the death. The young colts of his own herd have to keep apart from the mares, in a group by

themselves. The fillies do not stand to the stallion until their sixth year, but even so the instinctive aversion to inbreeding comes into play: when his own daughters come of age the stallion drives them out of the herd.[8]

This system was natural for a nomadic people living on a steppe-land. When the nomads entered the cultivated lands of Europe, the system had to be adapted to the new situation, though it would still have remained recognizable. Jankovich himself recalls how, as a boy in Hungary at the beginning of the twentieth century, he was entrusted with the care of fifteen half-grown colts at pasture:

> My terms of reference were precise: I was to keep them out of the sown and standing corn. Since grassland was not extensive with us, and surrounded by arable land, this was no easy task, and it was made more difficult by a penchant which the colts had to panic at the slightest sound, and, unaccustomed as they were to grazing in the open, to make off over hill and dale. Nevertheless, I managed to hold down the job of colt-herd for a long time, solely due to the fact that the leader of the herd was a three-year-old. It was simply a question of time before I managed to halter him and break him to ride. Once on his back I could easily lead the herd wherever I wanted it. On our migrations I always rode him in front, and my younger brother on a donkey whipped-in the stragglers. Later, when I became a breeder myself, I kept an old mare among the youngsters. With her help there was never any trouble, even on unfenced pastures.[9]

In England the landscape would have been different, but there would have been scope for such herds of horses in forests or moorland, or in parks which had been specially enclosed. Domesday Book (1086) contains many references to *equae silvaticae*, *silvestres* or *indomitae* (woodland or untamed mares). It must be presumed that the foals and fillies would run with their dams for a year, after which the owner of the herd would round them up so as to form them into a new herd. Jordanus Ruffus, writing in Italy in the mid-thirteenth century, said that they should be trapped in nets, either early in the morning or when the weather was cloudy, so that they should not damage themselves by struggling with increased desperation in the heat of the day. For the same reason he prescribed that the nets should be made not out of rope or hemp, but of wool. When the colts had been caught they were to be put in company with adult horses which had already been tamed 'since by nature everything longs for its like'.[10] This system continued much longer in some districts than in others, and still survives in the New Forest and on Exmoor and Dartmoor, but in general it was soon superseded by Stage 2.

Stage 2 consisted of a deliberate attempt to improve a breed by taking one selected stallion to as many groups of mares as possible in the three months of the breeding season. The reason for this, as the eighteenth-century breeder Robert Bakewell put it, was that

> even one superior male may change considerably the breed
> of a country. But in a year or two, his offspring are
> employed in forwarding the improvement. Such of his sons
> as prove of a superior quality are let out in a similar way;
> consequently the blood, in a very short time, circulates
> through every part, and every man of spirit partakes of the
> advantage.[11]

In the eighteenth, nineteenth and early twentieth centuries stallion owners would advertise in local newspapers, stating the date at which they would arrive at various market towns and the fee for covering a mare. Kings and nobles who owned several studs had circulated their best stallions round them for a long time. The earliest reference to the system in England is in the Pipe Roll or royal accounts for 1130 (the first to have survived) which records the payment of 30s. to Swein, the King's squire (*scutiger*), 'while he was at Gillingham [Dorset] with one stallion for covering the King's mares'.[12] If the King's mares had been a wild herd with a stallion of their own, the introduction of a second stallion would have led to a fight. It must therefore be assumed that the mares had been segregated and confined to a park, the essential feature of a park being that it was enclosed with palings sufficiently tall and strong to keep some animals in and others out (see pp. 80–81 below).

Stage 3 went further and involved the stabling of both stallion and mares. The reason for this was that a stallion put in with twenty mares might exhaust himself on the inferior mares, so that his covering of the better ones was unsuccessful. It was therefore best to keep him in a stable of his own where the mares could be introduced to him individually. Since it was essential to ensure that each mare was introduced only when she was in season, the mares had to be supervised with care. Hence the need for stables and a large number of stable-lads. It seems likely that this system had become the norm in England and most other parts of Europe by the beginning of the thirteenth century. The works involved were not elaborate and are illustrated by an instruction issued to the sheriff of Yorkshire in 1359:

> to cause the King's peel of Haverah [*Haywra*] called Skirgill with a brattice about the parapet [*barbettam*] thereof, to be maintained and repaired from time to time as may be necessary by the advice of Thomas [de Botha]; and an old house of Haverah in the park del Haye to be removed and to be renewed there for a stable; and a certain enclosure within the said park del Haye to be rebuilt, and another within the park of Haverah in which the King's mares may be covered [by the stallions]; and also a certain wall of earth about *le Horshous* within the park of Burstwick [*Brustwyk*], and an enclosure within that park in which the King's mares there may likewise be covered; and all other old houses and closes in those parks to be repaired.[13]

Since £268 had been spent making Haverah suitable for the King's mares some twenty to twenty-five years before, the expense of maintaining it was considerable.

It should be added that some people did not agree with the covering being 'in hand', considering it unnatural that both stallion and mare should be held by halters and assisted in the work.

William Cavendish described the method which he preferred:

> Put the *Stallion* to the *Mares*, thus: Take off his *Hinder Shooes*, and bring him near where the *Mares* are, and let him *Cover* a *Mare* in *Hand* Twice, which will make him *Wise*; and instantly Pull off his Bridle, and put him to the *Mares*: Which *Mares* must all be put in a Convenient *Closse*, that may *Feed* them *Well* for six *Weeks* at least.
>
> Put those *Mares* that have *Newly Foled*, and those that are *With Fole*, and those that are *Barren*, all to him; for there is no Danger in it. This Way is so *Natural*, as they are all Served in their *Height of Pride*; for, the *Horse* never *Mounts* them until they *Woo* him to it Extreamly.
>
> When he hath *Covered* them All, then he Tryes them all Over again, and those that will Take the *Horse*, he *Covers* them; and those that will Not, he lets them Alone: And when he knows he has Finished his *Work*, he beats the *Pale* to be gone, which is Time for him; then you must take him Up, and you shall find him Lean enough, nothing but Skin and Bones, and his Mane and Tayl will *Moot Off*. If you give him too many *Mares*, then he will serve you the Less time, be so Lean and Weak, that you will hardly Recover him against the next Year, or *Covering-time*. Therefore ten or twelve *Mares* is Enough.[14]

He added that it was necessary to have a man attendant on the stallion and mares constantly. A little hut was to be built for him and he was to be on the watch to see which mares were covered by the stallion, and to ensure that no other horse entered the enclosure.

Any breeder who wants to produce horses which are larger or smaller than the norm will not only choose his stallion and mare with care, but also regulate their diet. The genetic principle is the same for horses as for humans: a change of diet will not affect the height of anyone who is adult, but it will affect children. During the Second World War dieticians in Great Britain were so concerned with the possible effects of rationing that they prescribed special diets for expectant mothers and their children, and continued them after the war, with the result that children born then and subsequently grew noticeably taller than their parents. (My own sons went to the same schools as I did, but the desks which had been large enough for me were too small for them and their contemporaries.) Similarly the children born to Japanese immigrants to California almost inevitably grow taller than their parents. Horses increase in size most rapidly if bred in <u>fenland or watery pastures</u>, but since the growth is due to the amount of water in the grass, there is a danger that the horses concerned will outgrow their strength unless there is some compensating genetic factor or carefully selected supplementary feeding. The best grazing for building up bone is on <u>limestone or chalk</u>, because of the calcium in the grass. <u>Oats</u> provide an admirable all-purpose diet, but they can be expensive.

It is difficult to estimate the cost of breeding by any of the above methods, because it is extremely hard to give figures for the most important variable, which must have been the fertility or infertility of the mares. A mare's period of gestation is eleven months, so that, if one ignores the possibility of twins, one would have to reckon a foal a year as an absolute maximum. In fact a number of mares may prove barren. William Cavendish reckoned that if his mares were covered 'in hand' (method 3) the failure rate was about 50%, while by his own variant of method 2 it was reduced to about 1 in 6.[15] Among the feral mares of the USA the fertility rate is often around 60%, with quite a few of the mares producing a foal a year, and about 92% of the foals surviving their first year. It has also been found that the fertility of the mares can improve to almost 75% if the foals are removed from their dams in the autumn, because the dams, no longer having to nurse their foals, will be able to retain all the nourishment of the sparse grazing for themselves (see Appendix II, pp. 133–4).

Agricultural horses (*stotti*) in the Middle Ages received no such consideration. In the second half of the fourteenth century, which was a time of economic distress, they were often ill-fed, and the mares kept at work even when they were pregnant. The following figures come from two manors belonging to Battle Abbey in Kent.

YEAR	MARLEY FARM		BARNHAM	
	MARES	LIVE BIRTHS	MARES	LIVE BIRTHS
1352–3	13	2	7	2
1353–4	12	1	7	1
1355–6	11	5	—	—
1357–8	16	6	—	—
1358–9	13	1	6	1
1368–9	—	—	2	0
1384–9	7	2	—	—
totals	72	17	22	4

In 1353–4 it was explained that at Marley Farm 8 of the 12 mares were sterile, and that 3 others lay on their foals, while at Barnham the reason given for only one live birth was 'the great amount of work in the fields and with the men'. In 1357–8, 4 of the 16 mares at Marley Farm had miscarriages and 6 were barren.[16]

The fertility rate would obviously have been higher when mares were kept at stud, but the maintenance of a stud was very expensive. Compared with castle-building studs might at first seem cheap, but whereas a castle was a sound investment, because once it had been built it was an economical and labour-saving instrument for the subjugation or policing of a hostile territory, the running costs of studs kept on escalating. The enclosure of a park and the building of stables might not be too costly, but the more horses one bred, the more one had to spend on them. It cannot have been easy to find enough pasture, at any rate by the present-day standard of 4 acres (1.6 ha) for a mare and her foal, and the better quality horses had also to be fed on oats – we know that this was normal even at the beginning of the ninth century.[17] In the fourteenth century the normal diet of horses included oats, hay, beans, pease and straw. The cost of housing and feeding a good horse (including half a basket of oats a day) in 1314–15 varied according to season from $6\frac{1}{4}d.$ to $7\frac{1}{3}d.$ a day – and this at a time when a stable-lad would not receive more than 2d. a day, or a skilled mason more than 4d.[18]

44

It is not difficult to see that the costs of the studs could easily become ruinous, or that in years of plague or famine it might simply be impossible to find sufficient fodder. The problem would not have been so acute when the horses were employed in a war which was both successful and profitable, when the army was on the offensive in someone else's country, but as soon as peace was restored there was bound to be a cry for economy. That was when the investment of previous years was likely to be thrown away, because the obvious economy would be to sell off the horses and break up the studs. In that way one could obtain a supply of ready cash from sales, coupled with long-term economies from a greatly reduced payroll. The fact that one was likely to flood the market and get ridiculously low prices for the horses was doubtless regrettable. Far more serious was the fact that one might lose the breed entirely and find oneself back in the position of having once again to start building up a stud from the beginning. It must have been like a game of 'snakes and ladders', but it was what happened over and over again, not only in the Middle Ages but also in later centuries.

For the best documented examples of these booms and slumps it is necessary to go outside the Middle Ages. In his history of the English shire horse (first developed by Henry VIII: see below, pp. 108–9) Keith Chivers has shown a very clear sequence in the production of draught horses, revolving round three great wars, the Napoleonic and the First and Second World Wars.[19] The Napoleonic wars and their aftermath undid the work of Robert Bakewell, who had established his 'Dishley Breed' and introduced new standards of draught horse breeding throughout England. Europe suffered such heavy casualties of horses during the wars that European landowners, anxious to establish good breeds as quickly as possible, were extremely keen to buy draught horses from England as soon as the fighting was over (1815), and drove prices up so high that the English could not resist depleting their own stock seriously. Then followed the agricultural depression of 1820–32 which placed farmers in such financial difficulties that prices fell dramatically. In 1822 William Cobbett reported prices less than a third of what they had been in 1813. Four-year-old colts which had cost £25 to rear were sold for £15.[20] There was no longer any profit in good breeding so far as draught horses were concerned, and consequently standards plummeted. There was no serious improvement until the 1860s and 1870s.

It was much the same with the First World War (1914–18), which occurred shortly after the number of horses in Britain had reached its peak, calculated at 3.3 million, in 1901.[21] By 1914 the decline would have been noticeable only in large towns such as London, where horse-buses, horse-cabs and horse-carriages had been largely displaced by motor-buses, motor-cars and electric trams. During the war, however, the demand for draught horses increased enormously, since very large numbers were required by the army, motor-lorries of that time being unreliable in difficult terrain such as Flanders mud. As a result English farmers used every possible mare for breeding, while the government (unable to wait for the foals to be born and grow up) imported horses and mules from the USA at the rate of 1,500 a month. When the war came to an end, the army wanted to save the cost of stabling and fodder as soon as it possibly could. By March 1919 (only four months after the Armistice) it had sold as many as 62,500 horses on the open market in England, and this at a time when the number of English colts since 1914 must have been near its maximum. As a result prices collapsed. One breeder of shire horses had eight mares which he valued at £1,240 in 1920 and £300 in 1921, but sold in 1922 for only £82.9s.[22] And there was no prospect of any marked improvement, because in peacetime the number of horses required was diminishing steadily. Even on farms the horse population dropped from 960,000 in 1918 to 650,000 in 1939.[23] The number of new shire mares registered which had averaged 4,369 a year in 1915–21 dropped to an average of 1,943 a year in 1922–6, and 758 in 1931–4.[24]

At that point there was obviously a danger that the breed would be lost. It was in fact rescued by the efforts of the Shire Horse Society, a dedicated body of horse-lovers which organized much successful publicity, and succeeded in increasing the number of new shire mares registered in 1935–9 to an average of 1,019 a year. But that was only a temporary triumph. During the Second World War (1939–45) the need to produce more food quickly and with less labour made tractors essential, and when, after the war, tractors came onto the market in large numbers the plough horse was doomed. As the manufacturer of Ferguson tractors put it,

> On a ten acre [4 ha] farm, four had to feed the horse and the farmer had to work 1,000 hours to cultivate his land: with a Ferguson tractor he could do it in 200 hours, decrease his costs, keep more hens or extra pigs and cattle, and at the same time save his country.[25]

The logic of the economics was undeniable. Farmers bought tractors and sold off their horses so fast that the bottom dropped out of the market, and the only purchaser to be found was the knacker. It has been estimated that at least 100,000 farm horses were slaughtered in 1947, and another 100,000 in 1948, about 40% of them being less than three years of age.[26] As for the registration of new shire mares, it dropped to an average of 70 a year in 1960–64.[27]

That was the point at which the breed might have been extinguished. Once again it was rescued by the Shire Horse Society. The number of shire horses remains very small, but they have not declined further because they have been protected by the enthusiasm of horsebreeders who are moved by high sentiments rather than by economic considerations. This is a feature of horsebreeding which must not be forgotten. Some breeds are preserved for idealistic reasons. From the reign of Henry VIII the medieval warhorse was preserved for about a hundred years after it was really needed, because sufficient horsebreeders thought it looked more impressive or more beautiful than later breeds. It was only when they had become accustomed to the new breeds that they succumbed to economic realities, and allowed the medieval warhorse to disappear.

22 *Horses from Spain: an illustration of the Four Horsemen of the Apocalypse in a manuscript made c. 1109 for the abbey of S. Domingo de Silos, on the pilgrimage route to Compostela. It follows earlier illustrations (one of them made in AD 975) of the same text and is interesting for the non-Biblical emphasis it puts on the horses being spotted (cf. p. 59).*

3

The Revival of Horsebreeding in Western Europe, *c.* 700–*c.* 1400

We have seen in Chapter I how cavalry became important in Western Europe in the eighth century, and in Chapter II how the necessary breeds of horse, having reached the Mediterranean world by the fifth century BC, kept getting lost and having to be reintroduced. This latter fact explains how it was that in the sixth and seventh centuries of our era there was a certain amount of fighting on horseback, though not on a large enough scale to make the cavalry arm decisive. Similarly the earliest medieval references which we have to horses and horsebreeding suggest a haphazard state of affairs. Pope Gregory I (590–604) complained that the papal lands in Sicily were encumbered with 'herds of horses which we keep in a very useless state', and wanted to dispose of them, reserving 'only four hundred of the younger mares kept for breeding'. He had been sent one horse and five asses, but 'the horse I cannot ride because it is a wretch, nor the asses, good as they are, because they are asses'.[1] In North Italy the laws of King Liudprand (712–44) include strict regulations about the need for witnesses in horsedealing; because of the prevalence of horse-stealing it was not acceptable for anyone to say he had bought his horse 'from some Frank, or nobody knows whom'.[2] According to a *Life* written shortly before 769, St Corbinianus rode around Lombardy on a horse called 'Iberus' (the Spaniard), a stallion so beautiful that even the King coveted him. Eventually the animal was stolen and put to cover the King's mares, but God avenged his saint by striking the mares so covered (about forty-three of them) with a mortal disease, so that the guilty Lombard repented and paid the saint compensation in the form of two hundred silver shillings and two 'better' Spanish horses. This is the earliest medieval allusion to Spanish horses outside Spain.[3]

Spain had been conquered by the Moslems within ten years of their crossing from Africa to Gibraltar in 711. The Moslems were cavalrymen, as has already been mentioned, but they were not all Arabs. Though under Arabic rule, they were mostly Berbers (or Numidians) from North Africa, who had embraced Islam as soon as they had been overcome, and then joined the Moslem armies in order to share in future conquests. Their horses were probably of African origin (p. 37). The Greeks had acquired riding horses from Libya, and the Romans had racehorse studs for their chariot races in Algeria, while the neighbouring Numidians were well known for their cavalry. It may therefore be assumed that at this date also the North Africans had good riding horses of their own. It is thus likely that only a small number of horses in the Moslem armies which invaded Spain could have been Arabians, the legendary numbers given by Ibn Khalikan (who wrote five hundred years after the event) being that 'in the 12,000 Berber cavalry who disembarked in Spain under the command of Tarik there were only 12 Arabian horses'.[4] It must be said, however, that both Arab and 'Barb' horses are light, swift and capable of great endurance, that in any admixture of the two persistently skilled breeding could give a far greater emphasis to the Arabian strain than a comparison of total numbers might suggest, and that in any case either breed, or any combination of them, would be new in Western Europe. It could also be that the horses brought to Spain and Portugal by the Moslems were improved by cross-breeding with the horses which were already there. The elder Pliny, in the first century BC, referred to splendid horses in the region of Lisbon and the Tagus valley, but he did not add to the credibility of his statement with his claim that the mares were made pregnant by the west wind, and that the resulting offspring, though very swift, did not live longer than three years.[5]

We have already seen in Chapter 1 that Heinrich Brunner connected the emergence of large cavalry armies in Western Europe with Charles Martel's victory over the Moslems from Spain at the battle of Poitiers in 732. It is certainly round about that time that the Frankish armies are first seen to have really large bodies of cavalry. The American historian Lynn White Jr has suggested that they had previously been ineffective as cavalry because they had no stirrups until they learnt about them from the Moslems. It is true that a cavalry charge with lances couched would have been impossible without stirrups, but as we have seen above (p. 15) it is unlikely that such charges took place before the eleventh century, and in any case it is not certain when stirrups were introduced into the West.[6] Even if Lynn White was wrong about stirrups, however, Brunner's theory was probably right, since it was in the eighth century that the Franks discovered the Arabian horse.

The first specific evidence that the Franks not only knew about Spanish horses, but had actually captured a horse ridden by a Moslem warrior in Spain, comes in a document of about AD 795 in which Charlemagne states that he had received a letter from his son Louis (the Pious) with news of a victory over the Saracens of Barcelona, in which the spoils included 'a fine horse, a fine coat of mail and an Indian sword, together with a casket made of silver'.[7] Robert-Henri and Anne-Marie Bautier have collected many references to horsebreeding in North-West Spain in the ninth century, especially from cathedrals and abbeys on, or close to, the pilgrimage road to Santiago de Compostela; particular examples include an endowment of horses and mares for a priory of San Millán de la Cogolla, soon after 800, and (near the end of the ninth century) the dowry of a Galician lady which included twenty horses and thirty mares with their colts less than one year old. In 876 Pope John VIII wrote to the King of Galicia asking for some of the 'excellent Moorish [i.e. Berber or Barb] horses which the Spanish call *alfaraces*', *faras* being the Arabic word for horse.[8] In 883–7 when Notker wrote his (largely legendary) *Life of Charlemagne* he stated, and presumably found it plausible, that Charlemagne had sent a present of Spanish horses and mules to 'the Emperor of Persia', i.e. the Caliph.[9]

We know also that Charlemagne took a keen interest in horsebreeding. In his *Capitulare de Villis*, which dates most probably from the last years of the eighth century, it is stated that the stewards of the royal 'vills' or estates

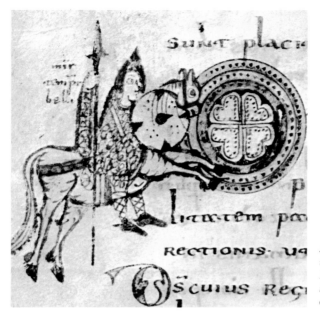

Within the image: SUNT PLACI... mir tempor bell... hatatem pa... RECTIONIS UA SCUIUS REGI

23 *A mounted Frankish warrior as illustrated in the Mass for those going to war in the Gellone Sacramentary, c. 790–95.*

(13) must take good care of the stallions [*equos emissarios, id est waraniones*] and under no circumstances allow them to stay in one pasture [*loco*] lest it be spoiled. And if any of them is no good [*quod non bonus sit*], too old or dead, the stewards are to see to it that we [Charlemagne] are informed at the proper time, before the season comes for sending them in among the mares [*iumenta*].

(14) must look after our mares well and separate them from the colts [*poledros*] at the proper time. And if the fillies [*pultrellae*] increase in number, let them be separated so that they can form a new herd by themselves.

(15) must have our foals at the winter palace at Martinmas [11 November].[10]

The implication of the regulation about stallions is that they were few in number but highly prized. This should not surprise us; we have already noted Robert Bakewell's dictum that 'even one superior male may change considerably the breed of a country', and if, as appears to have been the case, Charlemagne had segregated his mares so that none but his special stallions had access to them, the effect on the breed must have been significant. Charlemagne also put a prohibition on the export of stallions. In the Capitulary of Mantua, *c.* 781, stallions (this time called *amissarios*) are specified, together with female slaves and any sort of arms, as objects which were not to be sold outside the kingdom.[11]

It is difficult to say how much bigger were Charlemagne's horses than those which had been bred previously. Paul the Deacon, writing shortly before 800, believed that even in the sixth century the Lombards had coveted the 'herds of noble mares' which the Franks possessed, but it is only with Ernoul le Noir that size becomes a special feature of Frankish horses. In his adulatory poem on Louis the Pious (*c.* 826–8) Ernoul writes of horses which 'carry their necks proudly, and onto whose backs one could hardly mount', or 'with outstanding bodies such as the land of the Franks breeds'.[12] When one looks at the illustrations made at the time, however, they seem relatively small and lightly built.   23

The military importance of horses is recognized even more clearly in the Edict of Pîtres (864) issued by Charles the Bald when the West Frankish kingdom was suffering from the Vikings.

Since because of our sins the Northmen are coming into our district, and byrnies [coats of mail] and arms and horses [*caballi*] are either given to them as ransom for our men, or sold to them out of desire for money; as these things are given for the ransom of one man or sold for a small price, the result is that aid is given to those who are against us, very great damage is done to our Kingdom, many of God's churches are destroyed, many Christians are robbed, and the resources of the Church and Kingdom are exhausted . . . Therefore we decree that anyone who, after July 1st next of this indiction, should give a byrnie, or any sort of arms, or a horse to the Northmen, for any reason or for any ransom, shall forfeit his life without any chance of reprieve or redemption, as a traitor to his country, exposing Christianity to the heathen and perdition.[13]

We know that the danger of letting the Northmen acquire horses had been recognized years before. Ernoul le Noir had praised Datus, founder of the abbey of Conques, for his steadfastness in refusing to ransom his mother for a warhorse, even though the Northmen eventually killed his mother before his eyes.[14]

Horsebreeding was bound to be an important matter for any military power. The fact can be illustrated by the Saxons who had to bear the brunt of the Hungarian invasions in the tenth century. It was Henry the Fowler (918–36) who first organized a successful defensive strategy. His fortified towns were one part of his strategy, but less attention has been paid to the other part, which was the creation of a cavalry force. We know that slightly earlier (*c.* 903–6) there was a regular trade in horses which were brought by Slav merchants from Russia or Bohemia to Rafelstetten on the Danube near Linz; the toll levied for a stallion was one *tremiss* (the same as for a female slave) and for a mare one *saiga* (the same as for a male slave).[15] If, as is likely, it was impracticable for Henry to obtain horses by such a southerly route, his best hope would have been to capture horses from the Hungarians. It has sometimes been thought that the Hungarians' horses were large, the theory being that in their previous wanderings that people must have come across 'Bactrian' horses in the region north of the Caspian and Black Seas, but it now seems that their horses were small, probably derived from the primitive Tarpan horse of Asia, the average not being more than fourteen hands.[16] If Henry did capture some before 924, he would have been able to breed from them during the nine years' truce which he purchased. As Professor Leyser has shown, he certainly instituted studs (*equariciae*) and trained his men to fight as cavalry, though with such small horses it is hardly likely that they carried much armour.[17] It seems very possible that the Saxons and subsequent emperors used only small horses and light cavalry for longer than the Franks, and if this was in fact the case it may help to explain why the institution of knighthood developed in Germany only in the twelfth century, about a century later than in France, and why William of Apulia claimed that in the 1050s the Germans still preferred to fight on foot (cf. p. 60).

Saxons late
/ chivalry

In Western Europe the strongest military power to emerge from the wreck of the Carolingian Empire was that of the Normans. The Norman countryside is still known as good breeding ground for horses, and it is quite possible that the Carolingians had stud farms there, and that the Normans took them over. In spite of the Normans' reputation as destructive Vikings, it is now recognized that a greater number of Carolingian institutions was preserved in Normandy than in any other part of France. By the 1020s the dukes of Normandy were receiving many warriors into their service from outside the Duchy; they came from the Vexin, the Ile de France, Touraine, Anjou, Maine, Brittany and even Germany. These men, who soon joined the nobility of the Duchy, were presumably attracted by the opportunity of fighting many successful and profitable battles under the leadership of the Norman dukes, part of the attraction lying (it would seem) in the large number of good warhorses at the duke's disposal. That, at any rate, is the assumption underlying the (folkloric) story of Duke Robert the Magnificent (1027–35) and the smith of Beauvais, which was written down soon after 1087.

Duke Robert was generous not only with words but also with gifts, and if he made anyone a gift in the morning, he would keep on sending him everything that came to hand. One day a smith came from Beauvais [which was outside Normandy] and offered him two knives. The duke, not wishing to spurn the little gift of a poor man, accepted it gratefully, and told his chamberlains to give him 100 pounds Rouennais. The smith had hardly received the full sum when behold! two horses of outstanding strength appear; they had just been presented to the duke by two nobles, and the duke had ordered them to be given to the smith. The smith, afraid that he was being laughed at, was heartbroken and fell with his face on the ground, fearful that the magnificent gifts which the duke had given him would be taken back. At last, recovering his breath, he looked quickly to left and right, jumped on the back of one horse, grabbed the other

24 Drawing of a knight mounted on a spotted horse (compare Ill. 22), from a copy of the History of the Kings of Britain *composed by Geoffrey of Monmouth c. 1136, and transcribed at the abbey of Bec in Normandy shortly afterwards. The drawing stands at the beginning of the prologue addressed to Robert, Earl of Gloucester (d. 1147) and the horseman may therefore be presumed to represent him. He was quite well known to the monks of Bec, though the picture is probably both idealized and done from memory.*

with his right hand and returned to his city as fast as he could . . .

A year later, the smith returned to Normandy, bringing with him his two sons well instructed in arms, and coming before the duke, said 'Do you recognize me, your servant, O lord?' The duke said 'No'. And the smith replied, 'I am the man on whom you conferred magnificent presents last year, and I have come with my two sons to offer you faithful service, if Your Excellency will not refuse it.'[18]

Turning from myth to fact, it is clear that the Normans were accumulating valuable horses at least a generation before the conquest of England.[19] From the time of Robert the Magnificent onwards we read of highly-priced horses being offered in part payment for grants of land, either by noblemen such as Humphrey de Vieilles, or by monasteries such as Jumièges, Fécamp, Saint-Ouen-de-Rouen or Saint-Evroul. Since we know also that several nobles diverted the tithes of their mares from scattered parishes to abbeys such as Saint-Evroul (again), Saint-Georges-de-Boscherville, Saint-Amand-de-Rouen, Lyre or Saint-Sever, where they would be numerous enough to form a stud, we may suspect that monasticism and horsebreeding often went hand in hand. Between 1020 and 1054 Jumièges made four purchases of land for the price (among other things) of one horse worth 30 pounds,★ another worth 20 pounds, six horses of 'very great' and one of 'great' price. In the course of founding a priory at Saint-Gabriel, c. 1059–66, Fécamp paid out seven horses (two at 10 pounds, two at 7 pounds, and one each at 50 shillings, 42 shillings and 14 shillings 6 pence) and in addition made a loan of two more. When the most expensive horse is valued fourteen times higher than the cheapest, we can be sure the demand for quality is supreme.

An important factor in improving the strain must have been the acquisition of stallions from Spain. Some may have been brought back by Normans who, like Roger de Tosni c. 1023 or Robert Crespin in 1064, had fought for a year or two in the Spanish Reconquista. Others came as presents: William of Poitiers, writing

★ I use 'pounds', 'shillings' and 'pence' rather than '£', 's.' and 'd.' where the unit of currency is not the English pound sterling.

c. 1077, stated that in the late 1040s the great men of Gascony and Auvergne, and 'likewise the kings of Spain' sought Duke William's friendship with gifts of horses. With less authority, since it was written a hundred years after the event, the *Roman de Rou* stated that the horse which the Duke rode at Hastings had been brought from Spain by Walter Giffart. Gerald of Wales wrote (*c.* 1214) that Robert de Bellême introduced Spanish horses into Powys when he was Earl of Shrewsbury (1098–1102), and John of Marmoutier (*c.* 1162–71) that when King Henry I knighted Geoffrey of Anjou in 1128 he presented him with a splendid Spanish horse. After that examples could be multiplied. It is not surprising that the Bayeux Tapestry lays so much stress on the number and splendour of the Normans' horses.

4–6

The *chansons de geste* also are full of horses. Many of these, as we have already stated, came from Spain, but some were Gascon or, towards the end of the twelfth century, Syrian or Arabian. According to the *Song of Antioch* the Arab people were accursed of God – 'but what horses they have and what destriers of price!' In the *Song of Roland* (probably *c.* 1100) we are told the names of the horses of the principal characters, even, in some cases, of those of the Moslems. The names are usually descriptive. Count Gerin's horse was 'Sorel' (a bright chestnut colour), Gerer's 'Passecerf' (overtake the deer), Ganelon's 'Tachebrun' (brown spot) and Roland's 'Veillantif' (valliant). Charlemagne's 'Tencendur' (ash-grey) had been won by him, we are told, 'at the fords below Marsune, where he struck dead Malpalin of Narbonne', and may therefore have been Spanish. Archbishop Turpin's horse is not named but had been captured from a king killed in Denmark and is described as follows:

> A swift horse this and very fleet of foot,
> Its leg was slender and its hoof well arched,
> Short in the thigh and powerful in the croup,
> Long in the ribs and high along the back,
> A pure white tail he bore, a golden mane,
> Small ears upon his golden-coloured head;
> There was no beast that might compare with him.[20]

25 Archbishop Turpin and the Emperor Charlemagne (on the left) in a manuscript of Girard de Roussillon, c. 1200. The Archbishop is wielding a cross; the other figures have abandoned their lances and are engaging each other with swords in a general mêlée. One of the enemy, far right, is riding a spotted horse.

Among the most popular colours of horse in the *chansons de geste* were *liard* (silver grey) and *baucens* (skewbald, or white spots on some colour). These latter are illustrated so frequently in the manuscripts of Mozarabic Spain as to look almost like a trade-mark of Spanish horses, and it must be significant when we find Norman illustrations of similarly dappled horses.

While the Normans in France and the French generally were acquiring horses of African or oriental stock from Spain, those Normans who were in South Italy found a more direct route to the fountainhead of Barb and Arabian stock when, in the second half of the eleventh century, they conquered Sicily. Sicily had been under Moslem rule for two centuries and had strong trading links with Tunisia which the Normans retained. Though there is no specific evidence before the thirteenth century, it is inconceivable that the Normans did not acquire Barb and Arabian horses in this way. They were fortunate in having in Apulia and Calabria a terrain which was admirably suited to horsebreeding, since the limestone karst provided grass with plenty of calcium for building up the bones, while the stony surfaces of the rolling hills toughened the colts' hooves, strengthened their muscles and made them generally hardy. Certainly the Normans were very proud of their horses. Malaterra, writing soon after 1098, recounts how (reputedly in 1041) a Norman called Tuboeuf felled the horse of a Byzantine envoy with one blow of his fist, but then presented the envoy with a *better* horse for his return.[21] William of Apulia, writing *c.* 1095–9 about the battle of Civitate in 1053, claimed that the reason why Germans preferred to fight on foot was that they could not manoeuvre their horses so expertly as the Normans.[22] The Byzantine princess Anna Comnena states repeatedly that the Normans of Italy were invincible in a cavalry charge, and that her imperial father's tactic, at the end of the eleventh century, had been to make his men aim at their horses, since once on foot the Normans were very vulnerable, being hampered by the weight of their armour, while their huge shields and the spurs on their heels made them very clumsy.[23] According to the *Catalogus Baronum* of *c.* 1154–66, the number of knights owing military service in the Normans' Italian kingdom was 8,620, and we can assume that each knight had two or three horses at least.[24] Nonetheless there were evidently horses to spare because we find them being exported to France. In the *History of William Marshal* (written *c.* 1225) there is a description of a twelfth-century tournament in Champagne:

> La ve[i]ssiez chevals d'Espagne
> Porfichier la campagne
> de Lombardie et de Ceszire.[25]

(There you could see horses from Spain, Lombardy and Sicily being put through their paces.)

Leaving aside the reference to Lombardy, to which we will return later, it is important to examine the evidence for horsebreeding in Apulia and Calabria in the thirteenth century. The Emperor Frederick II (1212–50), who inherited the Norman Kingdom through his mother, was deeply interested in horsebreeding and had a large number of studs. In the records which have survived from his reign, we find him in 1239 instructing Paulinus of Malta to buy colts at Barca (near Benghazi) in Libya.[26] In the next year he is writing to Richard of Molise, his master-marshal in Sicily, confirming his order not to let his two Barb horses gallop until he has sent further instructions through Planerius, the squire (*scutarius*) of his marshalcy. In the event he instructed Planerius to bring the two Barb horses to his court; they were not to be ridden but led, Planerius himself being provided with a rouncy to ride, though his fellow-squire had to walk on foot.[27] Frederick was, and still is, renowned for his interest in science. He wrote a book on falconry which was full of personal observation, and he encouraged his staff to be equally scientific in their treatment of horses. In a later chapter we will have much to say about his knight-farrier, Jordanus Ruffus, who wrote *De Medicina Equorum* (On the Medicine of Horses) which was to prove a landmark in veterinary studies.

Some idea of the scale on which horsebreeding was practised in the Norman Kingdom can be gained from the last quarter of the

26 (far left) Norman knights portrayed on the north door of the church of S. Nicola at Bari in Apulia, almost certainly early twelfth-century.

27 (left) Coin of Roger I, Great Count of Sicily (1072–1101).

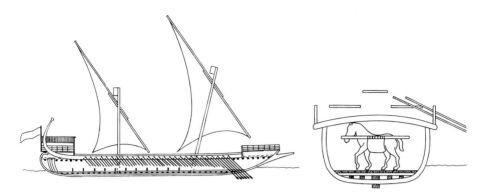

28, 29 Longitudinal and midships sections of a horse-transport, or tarida, built at Brindisi in Apulia in 1278 for Charles of Anjou. The drawings, by Dr John H. Pryor, are based on the evidence of detailed contracts for the vessels' construction.

thirteenth century when, with Frederick II defeated and dead, the Kingdom had fallen into the hands of Charles of Anjou (1268–85). Charles maintained the studs and enforced the rule that nothing be exported overseas without his licence. Unfortunately the registers containing these licences were destroyed in 1944, but recently Dr John H. Pryor has made a detailed study of the extracts printed in the nineteenth century, with the result that it can now be shown, for example, that in the year 1280 exports included one stallion, 64 warhorses and 808 other horses. The great majority of the ordinary horses were bound for Charles's overseas dominions or to his armies in Albania, but of the 64 warhorses 50 went to William de la Roche, Duke of Athens, and 8 to Guy de Tremolay of Chalandritza (in the Peloponnese), both of whom had recently become Charles's vassals. Pryor has also shown that the horses were shipped in special

28, 29   horse-transports called *taride*, each of which would carry about 40 animals. Their stalls were placed down the centre of the ship, and at right angles to its beam, so that the horses were facing one side or the other. In order to take the full weight off their legs, slings (*cynte*) made of canvas or rope were passed under their bodies.[28]

We know that horses from South Italy also reached North Italy and France. In the case of France the connection was probably King Charles himself, because he was intensely French and retained his counties of Anjou and Provence throughout his reign in Naples. In Italy he was the military leader of the Guelf (or papalist) party which had given him the moral and financial support necessary to win his Kingdom. He and his successors owed vast sums of money to bankers such as the Bonsignori of Siena and the Bardi, Peruzzi and Acciauoli of Florence, all of whom were rewarded with vast estates and generous commercial privileges. It would have been easy for them to buy horses in the South for sale in the cities of the North. Certainly Boccaccio (d. 1378) assumed that his Florentine audience would think it natural for a Perugian horsedealer in search of fine horses to set out for Naples.[29] It was not only that the quality of horses was particularly fine, but also that there was a very great number of them. An envoy from Barcelona to Naples wrote back to his employer 'we can hardly tell you how much going about on foot is looked down upon here [in Naples], for everyone rides a horse'.[30]

36

As we have already said, the main breeding grounds of South Italy were in Apulia and Calabria, where both the grazing on limestone and the nature of the terrain itself produced horses that were small, light, swift and strong, admirable for riding (palfreys) but not so good for service as warhorses (destriers). Since the great demand in the thirteenth century was not simply for warhorses but for larger and larger warhorses, enterprising horsedealers would have been very anxious to enlarge these Apulians. It seems that North Italians bought Apulian stallions, put them to larger mares, and kept them and their offspring on wet pastures where the large amount of water in the grass would cause the foal to grow bigger than his parents. The nearest precise evidence is in the chronicle by Gualvanei de la Flamma who reported as a novelty in 1341 that in Milan 'they put stallions in with great mares so that noble destriers were bred in our territory and fetched a great price'. He was probably wrong about the novelty. 'Horses from Lombardy', i.e. bought from Lombard merchants, first appeared (three of them) on the London market in 1232 and created quite a sensation. In November 1276 Nutus of Florence brought twenty horses for the English King and in the following January Donelin of Florence brought eighteen 'great horses' for the Welsh war. By the fourteenth century the references to Lombardy become more

63

insistent; in February 1309, for example, King Edward II sent Bynde Bonaventura and his brother Philip 'to the parts of Lombardy' to buy twenty destriers and twelve mares. At the time, the mares could only have been required for breeding.[31]

Exports from Italy into France have been studied by Robert-Henri and Anne-Marie Bautier.[32] They have shown how the numbers of horses involved can be related to the military activities of the French Crown, multiplying by ten in the years 1291–7 when there were wars in Guyenne and Flanders, and reaching another peak immediately after the disaster of Courtrai (1302). Taking all the Alpine routes together, they have reckoned that the number of horses imported into France from Italy reached a peak of 2,500 a year in 1296–7. In the years 1302–7 the volume was less, but still averaged 600–700 a year. It is not possible to say where exactly the horses came from, but it is sometimes possible to say where the merchants concerned originated. Taking the figures for two customs posts, Pont d'Ain and Châtel-Argent, for the periods September 1306–January 1309 and 3 July–23 November 1307 respectively, the numbers of horses being brought by merchants of named towns were:

from	Lodi	145	Parma	23
	Milan	81	Florence	13
	Bologna	42	Vicenza	13
	Piacenza	42	Verona	12
	Cremona	32	Crema	9

Italy was not the only source of supply for horses at this period. Spain was still a major producer, and we shall presently see that it exported horses to England in large numbers till the 1340s. From literary sources we know also that the French were importing horses from Holland, Frisia and Denmark in this period; bred mostly on fenland, they would have been large and would have contributed to the stock of great horses. It must be stressed, however, that the French did not acquire all their horses from abroad. The Crown did its utmost to increase the amount of horsebreeding in France itself. In 1279 King Philip III ordained that

30 *Warhorses as seen by a late fourteenth-century Lombard artist illustrating* Lancelot du Lac. *The horses provide the power, and the knights simply have to keep their lances straight and rigid (they are secured to the breastplate under the arm). Note also the high war-saddles. By this time Lombardy was a major European centre for fine horses.*

every knight or noble with 200 pounds worth of land and every bourgeois with goods or property worth 1,500 pounds should possess a brood mare; and that every baron, abbot, count or duke with sufficient pasture should have a stud of four to six mares by Candlemas (2 February) 1281.[33] Such measures were necessary in order to replace horses lost in war. Except in the rare eventuality of twins, a mare cannot produce more than one foal a year, and in normal conditions not more than nine or ten in her lifetime. Of these one might not survive more than a year, and others might not be of the required standard, so that the necessity of producing ever more horses of good quality, let alone of feeding them, must have seemed like a constant struggle against nature (cf. Appendix II).

Fortunately there was a demand for several alternative qualities. Though warhorses fetched the highest prices, other types were valued and came to be differentiated by special terms. In the twelfth century these terms are used only occasionally in chronicles or financial accounts, but it does happen that one of the most useful passages explaining some of the terms is a description of the horse market at Smithfield in the city of London, attached to a *Life* of St Thomas Becket written *c.* 1173–4:

> It is a joy to see the pacing horses [*gradarios*] with glossy coats ambling, that is to say, raising and putting down their feet on each side together. From here to see the horses [*equos*] more suitable for squires [*armigeri*]; they give a swift but roughish ride, raising and putting down their feet on opposite sides together. From here to the young 'noble' colts [*nobiles pullos juniores*] not yet fully broken in, 'high stepping and with elastic tread' [a quotation from Vergil's *Georgics*]. From here to the packhorses [*summarios*] with strong and active limbs. From here to the expensive warhorses [*dextrarios*] of elegant form and noble stature, with ears aquiver, necks upright and large buttocks. The purchasers watch them show their paces, first at a walk and then at a gallop, with their forefeet leaving and landing on the ground together, their rear feet also . . . There stand also the mares

31 The Lincolnshire knight Sir Geoffrey Luttrell, prepared for a tournament, c. 1340. His destrier is a 'great horse', and his lady has to stretch to hand him up his helmet. The elaborate trappings are more ornamental than functional.

[*equae*] suitable for ploughs, sledges and carts; the bellies of some are full with young.[34]

Medieval horses can be divided into four main classes, military, hunting, riding and agricultural. They are not always described by their technical terms – even the best were occasionally referred to simply as *equus* – but the prices paid for them are always a good indication, for which reason we give the general range to be expected *c.* 1250–1350. The best military horse was the warhouse or destrier (*dextrarius*) which would cost £50–100 or even more. The horse ridden by the non-knightly man-at-arms was a rouncy (*runcinus*) costing £5–10 or slightly more. The hobby, used (as we have already seen) by the light infantry, did not take part in the actual fighting and would probably cost about 40s. (£2). The best horse for hunting was a courser (*cursarius* or *fugator*) costing anything from £10 to £50. The courser was large as well as swift but for some reason does not seem to have been used for fighting. The most expensive horse for riding was a palfrey (*palfridus*), also costing £10–50. It was not necessarily very strong but had to be elegant and easy to ride; it was much in demand for state occasions. Some riding horses, including palfreys, were pacing horses which (as mentioned in the passage just quoted) moved both left feet forward together, and then both right feet, giving a very smooth and comfortable ride. There were – and still are – various terms for these horses: pacing horses (*gradarii*), amblers (*ambulatorii*), or trotters (*trottarii*). Hackneys (*haquenais*) make their appearance in the fourteenth century, but it is not certain whether they were necessarily pacing horses or just quiet ordinary horses. They would cost upwards of £3. Agricultural or peasant horses were much cheaper. A packhorse (*summarius*), which had many uses for the army and royal or noble householders as well as for lowlier folk, would cost between 7s. and 8s. A carthorse (*carectarius* or *veredarius*) or a peasant workhorse (*stottus* or *affer*) would cost about 2s.6d.[35] Thus a cheapish riding horse would cost 24 times as much as a peasant workhorse, a good palfrey 400 times as much, and a good warhorse 800 times as much.

32 *Battle scene from the* Pageant of the Birth, Life and Death of Richard Beauchamp, Earl of Warwick. *The Earl, who was Master of the Horse 1428–30, is shown on the left, with plumed helmet, in the act of routing the Dauphin's army.*

4

Horsebreeding in Medieval England

In the first three chapters of this book we have seen that the medieval warhorse did not conform to a fixed and immutable design, but was constantly being changed by selective breeding. The aim was to produce horses suitable for the military requirements of the day, but developing a new breed was a slow business, and military requirements kept changing. As in armaments industries, the difficulty facing horsebreeders was to produce what was required in sufficient quantity before it had become out of date. It was a difficulty which they must often have failed to overcome, but in general their achievements were remarkable. At the risk of oversimplification, they can be divided into four main stages.

(1) The production in large numbers of horses which, though small, were suitable for cavalry warfare. This was achieved between the middle of the eighth and the middle of the eleventh centuries.

(2) The rapid development of the size of the warhorse, so that it could carry armour of its own, as well as a more heavily armoured knight. This was achieved between the middle of the eleventh and the end of the thirteenth centuries.

(3) The age of the 'great horse', perhaps as tall as 17 or 18 hands. Fourteenth and fifteenth centuries.

(4) The decline of the 'great horse' and its gradual replacement by lighter breeds. Sixteenth and seventeenth centuries.

How closely was this general pattern followed in England? The answer to this question will necessarily be long and elaborate, because the amount of evidence available in England is far greater than anywhere else. No other country has a survey like Domesday Book (1086), or financial records (the Pipe Rolls) stretching in unbroken succession from the middle of the twelfth century onwards. No other country has, in relation to its size, so many title-deeds (charters) or government instructions such as are preserved in the Close and Patent Rolls. And though the financial records of the royal studs may not be as comprehensive as one might have hoped, they are far more complete than those of any other country.

Private records exist also, since most noble families and many religious houses had studs of their own. If we pay less attention to them than to those of the royal studs, this is simply because it would take more than a lifetime to work through them and sift out the relevant material. In any case the likelihood is that so far as warhorses were concerned, it would have been the king who set the example. It was he who knew when he wanted to make war and where, he who determined the quality of horses that should be brought to the army, he who had most opportunity and resources for the purchase of valuable horses from abroad, he who could control their import and export, and he who, in the last resort, could exercise a right of pre-emption. It was inevitable that he would be the leader in almost every new development, and that the nobles would follow his lead. Consequently there are sound reasons for concentrating on the royal studs. The number of horses which they produced would have been small when compared with the total output of all the private studs, but their significance was greater by far, because they would have set the trend.

THE ANGLO-SAXON PERIOD

We have seen that in Europe there was some sort of fighting on horseback in the sixth and seventh centuries A D but that it was only in the eighth century that cavalry was used in large numbers, the innovation being due to the Franks and probably connected with the discovery of Arabian or Barb horses from Spain. In England there was a similar development, but it may have occurred a good hundred years later, there being no firm evidence for a mounted army, as opposed to mounted individuals, before the reign of King Alfred (871–99).

Before the ninth century there is clear evidence for riding horses of good quality, as in the story told by Bede (d. 735) about King

Oswine (644–51) and St Aidan, who was his bishop. The King had given the Bishop a horse so that he could ride round his diocese. It was a special royal horse, and the King was much annoyed when he found that Aidan had given it to a beggar, for (as the King exclaimed) he had plenty of common horses which would have been more suitable for such a man.[1] Horses gave more than status: they also gave strength in battle. The date of the poem *Beowulf* is not known, but it probably belongs to the seventh or eighth centuries. It contains the following lines:

> Then the defence of warriors commanded eight steeds with gold-plated bridles to be led into the hall through the precincts. On one of them lay a skilfully decorated saddle enriched with jewels: that had been the high-king's war-seat when Healfdene's son wished to take part in the play of swords; the valour of the far-famed man never failed at the front when the slaughtered were falling.[2]

There is an interesting passage also in the law of King Ine of Wessex (*c.* 688–94) which states the compensation if anyone lends a sword, spear or horse to another man's *esne* who then runs away.[3] The text makes it clear that the value of a horse was twice that of a spear and three times that of a sword, but we are left guessing who or what was an *esne*. A slave would not have been equipped with sword and a freeman would surely have been responsible for his own actions. Neither slave nor free, he most resembles the 'man', 'young man' or vassal of the earliest stages of Frankish feudalism (above, p. 12).

In the Danish invasions of the ninth century we hear a lot more about horses. The general aim of the Danes (or Vikings) was to arrive by sea, surprise an undefended town, plunder it and sail away before an army could be raised against them. Their ships gave them all the mobility they required on water, but if they were to extend their activities inland they needed horses. We have already seen that the Frankish kings were aware of this danger and issued laws and injunctions to prevent anyone selling or giving them horses, even as ransom or tribute (above, pp. 53–4). Nonetheless the Danish raiders did obtain horses both from the Franks and from the English. In

England a charter of King Ceolwulf II of Mercia reveals that until 875 the obligation of feeding the king's horses and those who led them had been laid upon all the minster churches of the diocese of Worcester;[4] and if we suppose that the general principle was the same in the other English kingdoms and dioceses, it is not hard to see how the Danes succeeded. They would not have had to look for horses all over the country, but simply to make for the nearest minster church, seize it and hold its clergy and people to ransom for horses. Without explaining this, the *Anglo-Saxon Chronicle* makes a point of stating where and when the Danes succeeded in getting horses. It records that in 866 the Danes wintered in East Anglia and obtained horses there (*þaer gehorsade wurdon*), making it clear that that was the beginning of the Danes' serious campaigning in England.[5] In 876 a Danish army which occupied Wareham in Wessex somehow obtained horses and rode on to Exeter; the acquisition of horses within Alfred's own kingdom must have been regarded as shaming, because the fact is referred to again in the annal for the subsequent year. In 881, when the Danes were transferring their attention to the Continent, the *Chronicle* tells us that they moved inland from Ghent, won a battle and obtained horses, after which their activities extended deep into the Frankish Empire. When, in 885, they attempted a return to England they were cornered at Rochester, and though they managed to withdraw by sea, they were deprived of their horses (*hi wurdon þaer be horsade*). When they next returned to England, in 892, they brought their horses with them; the *Chronicle* specifically states that they had obtained sufficient ships in Boulogne to cross the channel in one journey 'horses and all'. In the subsequent campaigns they rode right across England on several occasions. When cornered and besieged in the west at Buttington-on-Severn they were reduced to eating most of their horses.

With the *Chronicle* paying such attention to the horsing of the Danes, it is not surprising to find references to the fact that the English army also was mounted. When King Alfred pursued the Danes from Wareham to Exeter in 877 he rode (*rad*) after them, as also after his victory at the Battle of Edington in 878. When the

Danes rode across England, twice in 893 and once in 894, Alfred's forces were able to pursue them effectively; and in case anyone might suppose that they did so without horses, we are expressly told that when they were besieging the Danes in Chester, they deprived them of provisions, wasted the land all round, and 'burnt all the corn or consumed it by means of their horses'. It is likely that King Alfred's mounted forces were connected with the 'king's thegns' who became prominent in his reign. It is then that we first hear of 'the king's horse-thegn'; he was obviously an important royal officer, because the deaths of two horse-thegns in succession, Ecgwulf and Wulfric, are reported at the beginning and end of the annal for 896.[6] Subsequently the title of the office was to change, to 'staller' (see pp. 76–7), but the mere fact of its existence in the ninth century is important. The Franks had a similar official called the _comes stabuli_ or constable.

The English kings were very much influenced by the Franks at this time. They were the two peoples who bore the brunt of the struggle against the Vikings, and the _Anglo-Saxon Chronicle_ reports the movements of the Danes within the Frankish kingdom with care and precision. There are many parallels in the laws of the two countries. In particular the decree of Alfred's grandson, King Æthelstan (925–39), that every landowner should provide two well-mounted men for every plough in his possession, is a clear variation of Charlemagne's requirement that every free man with four manses of land should equip himself for battle; and Æthelstan's prohibition against sending a horse overseas except as a present echoes Charles the Bald's prohibition against giving or selling horses to the Northmen.[7]

From the middle of the tenth century references to valuable horses become increasingly common in England. The king's earls and thegns owed him a 'heriot' (or death-duty due to one's lord) of which an important part was paid in horses. About 946–7 the Ealdorman Æthelwold in his will stated his heriot to be four swords, four spears, four shields, four bracelets, four horses and four silver cups.[8] About 946–51 the Ealdorman Ælfgar in his will left his lord two swords with sheaths, two armlets and three

33 Detail from the will of the Ætheling Æthelstan, c. 1014–15, recording the following bequests (underlined): 'a black stallion', 'my horse with my harness', 'a[nother] horse', and 'the stud which is on Colungahrydg'.

33   stallions, three shields and three spears.[9] About 1014–15 the Ætheling Æthelstan left a coat of mail and two horses (one of them white) to his father King Æthelred, a black stallion (*stedan*) to the Bishop of Winchester, a horse with harness to his chaplain, a pied stallion to his steward, and his stud on Colungahrycg (wherever that may have been) to his staghuntsman.[10] About 1008–12 Alfwold Bishop of Crediton left four horses to the King, two of them saddled and two not (the equivalent of the heriot of a king's thegn), and his wild mares (*wildra werfa*) at Ashburn to the King's son. In addition he left nine other horses to nine named individuals, one a monk and one a priest, and to each of his retainers (*hired men*) the horse which he had lent him.[11] About 975–1016 Ælfhelm, an important man in East Anglia, left half his stud (*stodes*) at Troston in Suffolk to his wife and half to the companions (*geferan*) who rode with him.[12] Similarly in 1043–5 Thurstan son of Wine left his stud at Ongar in Essex to his men (*cnihtes* – a word that Stenton (of whom more below) has taught us not to render as 'knights').[13]

Most important, however, is the statement about heriots in the laws of King Cnut (*c.* 1023). An earl's heriot is there reckoned at eight horses (four saddled and four unsaddled), four helmets, four coats of mail and four swords, together with eight spears and eight shields. The simplest explanation is that the lord was expected to have three fully armed companions, and that he and they were to have two horses each, one for riding and the other for battle. The additional four spears and four shields would have been for the four

74

men who led the warhorses when they were not being ridden by their masters in battle. The heriot which the law specifies for a king's thegn implies that he also would have had a warhorse as well as a riding horse: it consisted of four horses (two saddled and two unsaddled), one helmet, one coat of mail, two swords, and four spears and four shields. The assumption must be that a king's thegn had a single companion whom he supplied with horses and weapons but not with armour.[14]

The implication of the wills, like that of Cnut's laws, is that, at any rate from the middle of the tenth century, lords provided their men with mounts, which they might eventually make over to them as gifts. The same suggestion emerges from the poem *The Battle of Maldon*, written at some date after 991. The battle itself was fought on foot, but the poet complains bitterly of the flight of Godric son of Odda who 'forsook the hero [Brihtnoth] who had given him many a steed, . . . leapt upon the horse that had been his lord's, on the trappings to which he had no right', and galloped away giving many of the army the impression that it was not he but his lord who was fleeing.[15] It looks as if the lord's horse must have been adorned with special colours or insignia as in the later Middle Ages.

Till recently the orthodox view was that though the Anglo-Saxons rode to battle on horseback, they always dismounted to fight. There was nothing ridiculous about this because, as we have already seen, fighting on horseback was possible only if one's mount had been specially bred and trained as a warhorse. Sir Frank Stenton regarded this concept as fundamental and made it the basis of his argument that there was no feudalism in England before the Norman Conquest. He agreed with the general view that feudalism was a word used to describe a society based on fiefs, but he insisted that a fief was land given in return for military service *as a mounted knight*, part of the definition of a knight being that he was equipped and trained to fight on horseback. Therefore if there were no mounted knights, there were no fiefs and no feudalism.

In the last forty years many attempts have been made to overthrow Stenton's argument, the most important of them from our point of view being that of Richard Glover who, in 1952, argued forcefully that in fact the English did fight on horseback before the Norman Conquest.[16] Since then most scholars have treated the question with caution, the lack of evidence making a firm conclusion impossible. There simply is no reliable information about how the English fought in battle. But if we change the question slightly and ask if the English had warhorses before the Norman Conquest, an answer is possible and must surely be 'yes'. The English probably did not have as many warhorses as the Normans, and it may well be that their quality was not as good either, but what evidence there is all points to the fact that they existed.

The English also had an important official called the 'staller'. Stenton taught us to believe that this official was someone with a 'stall' or important seat in the king's hall, and therefore could be 'anyone with a permanent and recognized position in the King's company'.[17] The authority he cited was L. M. Larson, who had argued the stallership was 'Norse in name and origin, and that it came into England with the Danish host' of King Cnut.[18] The early instances to which Larson referred, however, derive from sagas written either *c.* 1190 or in the fourteenth century, or, so far as England is concerned, a charter which is now recognized as a forgery. In her edition of *Anglo-Saxon Writs* Dr F. E. Harmer showed that the office of staller first appears at the beginning of the reign of Edward the Confessor, who came to the throne in 1042.[19] Since Edward had spent the previous twenty-eight years of his life as an exile in Normandy, it is hard to believe that either title or office was of Norse origin rather than an anglicization of the Frankish and Norman *comes stabuli*, 'count of the stable' or 'constable'. According to Larson a Norse staller was 'the King's spokesman at the popular assemblies'.[20] None of King Edward's stallers can be seen to have performed this function. Eight of them are known (three or four of them serving at any one time) and of these one, Eadnoth, must have had military duties since he was killed leading an army against Harold's sons in Somerset in 1067.[21] Another, Robert fitz Wimarc, is described in the *Vita Edwardi Regis*

34, 35 *Two details from Domesday Book showing references (underlined) to the same man, identified once as 'Bondi stalrus' and once as 'Boding constabularius'.*

(written between 1066 and 1070) as *regalis palatii stabilator* which, since this text is often corrupt, is presumably a mistake for *stabularius*.[22] A third, Bondi or Boding, is described in Domesday Book as both *stalrus* and *constabularius*.[23] And a fourth, Ralph the Staller, held five villages in Kesteven, Lincolnshire (Hough-on-the-Hill, Brant Boughton, Fulbeck, Leadenham and Bennington), which had the unusual distinction of owing, between them, 300s. (£15) a year for horse-fodder (*ad victum equorum*).[24]

    If we consider the introduction of stallers together with the evidence of the heriots, it becomes extremely difficult to argue that the use of warhorses in pre-Conquest England was either unknown or totally different from that of Northern France or Normandy. Since the evidence begins much later in England than in France, in the ninth or tenth century rather than the eighth, it could be that horsebreeding had not been brought to the same peak of efficiency as in Normandy, but we have to hope that archaeology can produce some results. The earliest horseshoes to have been found in established contexts in England date from the ninth and tenth

34
35

centuries and have an overall width of $3\frac{7}{8}$ inches (100 mm), which indicates a small horse. Those from mid to late eleventh-century contexts average 4 inches (102 mm), sometimes being as wide as $4\frac{3}{8}$ inches (110 mm), while those from the later fourteenth century onwards have an average width of $4\frac{3}{8}$ inches and shoes $4\frac{1}{2}$–$4\frac{3}{4}$ inches (115–120 mm) wide are 'not uncommon'.[25] These facts confirm the general impression given by the historical evidence, but also point to a further *desideratum*. What we really need to know is the type of horse to which any shoe belongs. Those described above come from sites in London and should not be associated with warhorses. The best guess must be that they were intended for packhorses, but alternatively they might have been for small riding horses.

FROM 1066 TO *c.* 1280

We have seen that the Normans were famous for their horses and cavalry, and so proud of them that in the Bayeux Tapestry they hardly indicated the infantry at all, even though it certainly played an important part in the Battle of Hastings. We do not know the actual numbers involved in that battle, but the accepted guess of modern scholars is about 8,000 men, of whom 2,000–3,000 would have been cavalry. Though the cavalry may have formed little more than a quarter of the total number of effectives, they were by far the most expensive element in the army. In an impressive paper on the logistics of the Hastings campaign, Bernard S. Bachrach has reckoned that the *daily* ration for 2,000–3,000 horses 'weighing no less than 1,300 lbs. [590 kg] each' would have been in the region of 14–20 tons of grain (oats or good barley) and about the same amount of hay. This estimate is too high, and the totals extrapolated from it several times too high.[26] Even if we accept a total of as many as 2,000–3,000 horses, the evidence of the Bayeux Tapestry and the very wide range of prices for Norman horses (above, p. 57) suggests that only a few (perhaps a very few) of them would have reached the proposed weight of 1,300 lb or the height of 14 hands. Resisting the temptation to indulge in further statistics of the unknown, I would simply guess that the daily requirement of the army for its horses could not have been more than 10 tons of grain and 10 tons of hay. Even that amount could not have been produced without difficulty, and while the Norman army was living 'off the country' in England its horses must have created much havoc.

The Hastings campaign and subsequent punitive expeditions such as the 'Harrying of the North' (1069) were such disasters for the English people that in any context except that of this book it might seem frivolous to insist that they would also have delivered a severe blow to the English studs. Quite apart from the ruination of park fences, the shortage of fodder would have been extreme, since it was almost all being seized by the Normans. Thus the Conquest brought no immediate improvement to horsebreeding in England. That had to wait for the second generation of Normans; we recall that according to Gerald of Wales it was between 1098 and 1102 that Robert de Bellême introduced his Spanish horses into Powys (above, p. 58). The one improvement suggested by Domesday Book (1086), that Godric the sheriff had abstracted 43 acres (16 ha) from the royal demesne at Kintbury in Berkshire for the pasture of his horses, cannot refer to an event after the Norman Conquest, because Godric was one of the English killed at the Battle of Hastings.[27]

In 'Great' Domesday no figures are given for livestock, but these had been demanded in the original inquest and have been preserved in the circuit returns which cover Norfolk, Suffolk, Essex, Cambridgeshire, Dorset, Somerset, Devon and Cornwall:[28]

	NORFOLK	SUFFOLK	ESSEX	CAMBS.	DORSET	SOM.	DEVON	CORNWALL
rouncies	767	527	793	170	123	448	159	21
horses	50	127	3	—	—	—	—	—
mares	56	—	21	11	13	35	1	12
wild or forest mares	139	114	—	24	12	356	317	410
foals	25	—	103	7	12	—	—	—

Allowances have to be made for inconsistencies between the various commissions (covering East Anglia, the South-West and Cambridge) and for the fact that the Cambridgeshire figures have been taken from two different copies of the 'original returns' (*Inquisitio comitatus Cantabrigiensis* for the southern part and *Inquisitio Eliensis* for the north). Obviously those in the South-West and Cambridgeshire did not distinguish between 'rouncies' and 'horses'. In East Anglia horses (*equi*) were regarded as superior to rouncies, and the number of rouncies makes one wonder whether the word here denotes a farm horse rather than a cheap riding horse.

Wild or forest mares (*equae silvestres, silvaticae* or *indomitae*) were herds of mares which would run loose with a stallion in a forest or park as described in Chapter 2. They represented the simplest and crudest form of breeding (see pp. 38–9), the only human intervention being to round up the foals once a year. It is not always possible to see their general geographical pattern. The most important groups of them in Devon are on Exmoor, but in most counties the distribution has to be explained in detail. In Surrey, in Kingston Hundred, we are told that Walter fitz Other held one man to whom he had committed the charge of the King's forest mares;[29] Walter was castellan of Windsor, and presumably these forest mares could have been connected with those of Windsor Forest. In Norfolk where the forest mares were mainly on the Greensand Belt, Breckland or at the northern extremity of the Broads, the total number dropped, most surprisingly, from 359 in 1066 to 139 in 1086. The reason for this must have some connection with Roger Bigod, who held all three manors which registered decreases – Pentney, where the number of forest mares dropped from 20 to 7; Sutton, where it went down from 23 to 7; and Hockham (in Breckland), where it went from 220 to none.[30] Roger was sheriff of the county and it may be that he used his influence to persuade local juries to turn a blind eye to this part of his moveable wealth.

Domesday Book also lists thirty-five parks, some of which may have been connected with horsebreeding, though unfortunately it is not always possible to tell which. A park (*parcus*) was basically an enclosure for animals. In the ninth century the word could be used for an enclosure as small as a sheepfold or farmyard, but later it denoted a much larger area. Surrounded by hedges or fences, it was a place where one could 'park' animals in the same way as nowadays we 'park' our cars. The animals parked could be wild beasts for the chase, and in thirteen instances this is said to have been the case, but the later evidence suggests that many parks could have been for studs. Stoke Park at Guildford in Surrey, for example, played an important part in the royal studs in the fourteenth century, as also did the royal parks at Woodstock and Windsor. Three of the Sussex parks recorded by Domesday (at Waltham, Tortington and Walberton) may be thought to have been studs because their situation on the South Downs would have been admirable for horsebreeding.[31]

In the next century the information becomes more specific. Burton Abbey had a stud (haraz) with 70 mares and foals before 1114, and 85 mares at Whiston in Penkridge, Staffordshire, either at the same time or very shortly after.[32] In 1115 Walter de Gant gave to Bardney Abbey (Lincolnshire) pasture for 20 mares at Grinton in Swaledale, North Yorkshire.[33] Before 1121 a certain Hunoldus gave Shrewsbury Abbey the tithes of his forest mares at Upton Magna and Lustney in Hodnet, Shropshire.[34] In 1130 (as already mentioned) the King had mares at Gillingham in Dorset and arranged for his stallion to be taken to cover them there.[35] Before 1172 Roger de Mowbray had given the monks of Byland (in North Yorkshire) pasture for 70 mares and their foals in Nidderdale.[36]

The Pipe Rolls show that in 1164–5, when Archbishop Thomas Becket was in exile, the King allowed the sheriff of Kent 43s.6d. for the maintenance of the Archbishop's stallion and groom, and in the following year had some of his stallions and mares taken to the royal park at Clarendon in Wiltshire, and allowed 10s. for the enclosing of the Archbishop's park at Aldington in Kent.[37] Also in 1165–6 the sheriff of Shropshire had bought 15 horses from the stud (haracio) of Gervase Goch, Gervase being the third son of Meredith ap Blethyn, Prince of Wales, and tenant of the Shropshire manor of Sutton Maddock, now part of Telford.[38] Welsh horses already had a good reputation; in 1176 Philip fitz Stephen purchased the farm of Ackleton in Worfield, Shropshire, for 10 marks and one Welsh destrier.[39] We also read of the King's studs in Devon and Cornwall,[40] and that of Earl Conan of Richmond in Yorkshire, his estates having fallen into the King's hands.[41]

The King received many good horses in part payment of amercements (which we would now call fines) or reliefs (death-duties), but the way in which they were combined with other payments often makes it difficult to calculate their exact price. When it can be established, it appears that prices for each type of horse varied according to their individual quality. In the reign of Henry II (1154–89) a *fugator* or courser would probably have cost between 20s. and 30s., the same as a palfrey (though a special white palfrey for the papal legate in 1177 cost 33s.), and a destrier anything between 30s. and 60s., or in special cases more. One often finds, however, that the type of horse is not specified beyond phrases such as 'a very good horse' or 'a horse of great price', and in fact the most expensive beast (presumably a destrier), costing £6.13s.4d., is described simply as a 'horse'.[42]

The 'normal' warhorse seems to have been valued by the King's government at 40s. That, at any rate, was the usual price paid when 26 horses were purchased in sixteen different counties for the invasion of Ireland in 1171–2.[43] We do not know how many horses were taken on that campaign, but 390 certainly, and perhaps as many as 496, were shipped back.[44] There is no way of telling whether these latter included horses bought or captured in Ireland itself; if they were, they could probably have been small like the 'hobbies' of the fourteenth century (see p. 26).

It is often supposed that Arabian horses must have been brought back to England (and Europe also) by returning Crusaders, and in this connection King Henry II's son, Richard Coeur de Lion (1189–99), is often mentioned. It is known that in 1192 he was presented with two Arabian horses by Saladin's brother, El-Adil Seyf-ed-Din. It is not known, however, whether they were brought back to England. Richard certainly had horse transports – on the way out his horses had suffered from being a whole month at sea before they

36 Horses and their grooms. Stallions could be very troublesome with each other and usually required one groom for every two horses (if not for every one), as opposed to one for every three as shown here. From a manuscript made between 1352 and 1362 for Louis II, titular King of Naples. (Naples was known for its horses: see p. 63.)

reached Cyprus – but if the two Arabians were brought back in this way, it has to be admitted that there is no trace of them in the English royal records.[45] They may have been captured with the King in Austria in the course of his return.

It is in the reigns of John (1199–1216) and Henry III (1216–72) that we first get a glimpse of the administration involved in the management of the royal horses. In John's reign the key figure was Thomas de Landa. It is possible that Thomas owed his position to his elder brother Richard, but in 1207 he was one of the keepers (*custodes*) of the King's horses, with the title of *scutarius*, which means literally 'shield-bearer' but was applied to an officer in charge of horses. Though the number of keepers was about a dozen, Thomas seems to have had wider responsibilities than the others, because his name is mentioned far more often than theirs. In 1205 he was paid 20s. for a cloak, which indicates that he had superior status. In 1206 he took nine horses to Dorset, and in April 1207 three destriers with three lads (*garciones*) to Bristol, himself riding a rouncy. In October 1207 he was taking one of the King's horses to Bristol, and in September 1208 one sick and one healthy horse from Clarendon to Bristol.[46] In 1211–12 he was with Thomas the Farrier (*marescallus*) in Yorkshire, and also spent fifteen weeks from November to February with six destriers and seven lads in Northamptonshire, where, later in the same year, he is found again with fifteen horses and eleven lads. In August 1212 he was with twenty-eight horses and twenty-seven lads at Worcester.[47] In September 1213 he was in Yorkshire with seven horses and six lads. In the winter of 1213–14 he was in Kent organizing the horses for the King's crossing to France. In November 1214 he was taking horses to Wilton in Wiltshire and in December to Tewkesbury. From 27 December 1214 to 7 January 1215 he was with six of the King's destriers, one mule and two rouncies in Berkshire. On 26 January 1215 he was ordered to hand over to William Harcourt the dapple-grey horse, complete with harness, which had belonged to Hugh IX de Lusignan, with whom King John had just made peace. In February he was in Berkshire, presumably at Windsor, with eleven destriers, their eleven keepers, two horses and one lad, and that same year he was expected at London with three of the King's horses and one of his own. In March 1215 his brother Richard was one of the three men in charge of the King's Spanish horses (*equis nostris de Yspania*) at Northampton.[48]

Some officials were called 'marshals'. The Latin *mariscalcus* (or *marescallus*) is derived from two Germanic words, *marchaz* and *skalkaz*, denoting 'horse-servant'. The Frankish and French kings had marshals as officers subordinate to the constable or *comes stabuli*, as also did the Normans both in Normandy and in England. The chief marshal's office gradually rose in social esteem, the Earl Marshal, as he was called (from the fourteenth century), having little to do with the king's horses. But at a lower social level the word retained the original meaning of 'horse-servant' and was applied to the farrier or smith who is still known in France as *le maréchal* or *le maréchal-ferrant*. It also denoted a horse-doctor. The most famous horse-doctors in medieval Italy called themselves 'marshals', and in England a sick horse which needed a cure and recuperation was sent to be 'marshalled and renovated' (*marescalciari et renovari*).[49] Yet other marshals were neither smiths nor horse-doctors but in charge of the king's horses generally, supervising their maintenance, selling those that were not required and buying new bloodstock. The first definite marshals of this sort were Richard the King's marshal, *c.* 1232–41, and Ellis of Rochester, *c.* 1257–69. Ellis had as subordinates William de la Forde, keeper of the King's destriers, and Thomas de Tytellington, keeper of the King's palfreys.[50]

During this period there were some notable purchases of foreign horses, especially from Spain. Since the king of England was also duke of Aquitaine from 1152 to 1453, access to Spain was not difficult, and the horses bought were shipped to England from La Rochelle (till 1228) or Bordeaux. Many of the horses bought in Aquitaine itself may have been of Spanish origin. In 1242 the King sent Bernard son of William de Banares to Castile in order to buy horses there, and in the year following he paid the provost of Roncesvalles (on the frontier of Navarre) 100 marks for destriers which he had bought from him. In 1242 he also instructed the men of Bordeaux to seize a ship known to be sailing from Spain to La Rochelle (which by then was French) with a cargo which included horses.[51]

Though Spanish horses were still the most important in England throughout the thirteenth century, Lombard horses were beginning to make their appearance. As we have seen (p. 63), they are first mentioned in the records in 1232 when some were put on sale in London, and the King wrote to the mayor and sheriffs ordering them to help Richard his marshal to buy them at a reasonable price. Nine years later the same Richard was one of two agents provided with 1,000 marks for purchases at Lagny-sur-Marne.[52] This was one of the biggest of the fairs of Champagne where Italian merchants did most of their trade with Northern Europe, and since it is known that in general their trade included horses, it must be assumed that horses were what the King's marshal had been sent to buy.

Henry III's reign ended in civil war which must have done much to disrupt the studs. It is true that the barons were anxious to get horses for themselves – in 1260 Ellis of Rochester was ordered to seize three destriers imported into Dover by Simon de Montfort[53] – but the passage of warring armies, the various transfers of power, and the constant shortages of money must have led to a loss of efficiency. Circulating the right stallions to the various parks cannot have been easy in these circumstances, and the proper maintenance of park fences may well have been neglected, so that by the time of Henry III's death in 1272 a situation which should have been full of promise for horsebreeders must have become extremely disappointing.

FROM c. 1280 TO 1509

From the reign of Edward I (1272–1307) our knowledge of the royal studs is transformed, because separate accounts were kept for the *Equitia* (horse-business) from 1282 onwards. More strictly speaking we should say that our knowledge of the studs *will* be transformed when someone has found the time and patience to analyse the four or five hundred rolls or files which cover the period from 1282 to 1623. But even without a detailed analysis one very obvious fact can be observed – that in the main series of 415 items, 343 belong to the first 80 years (1283–1363) and only 72 to the remaining 261 years. There are reasons for thinking that this contrast may have been exaggerated by administrative changes which resulted in some of the expenditure on horses being recorded elsewhere. This is particularly the case in the Tudor period, since there are no special *Equitia* accounts for 1459–80 or 1484–9 and virtually none for 1490–1531 either. But for the greater part of the period from 1282 to about 1458 there is no serious cause for suspicion, and what is remarkable is the cyclical pattern of peaks and slumps, very similar to those we have seen in regard to the shire horse in the nineteenth and twentieth centuries. Edward I, Edward II and Edward III all started their reigns with *Equitia* expenditure at a low level, proceeded to increase it dramatically, and then suddenly let it drop again. The peaks were in the years 1292–1301, 1312–26, and 1337–61; and the slumps were in 1307–11, 1327–31 and from 1362 onwards. Although at first these fluctuations may appear surprising, it requires only a little thought to show that they are reflections of the political realities of the time.

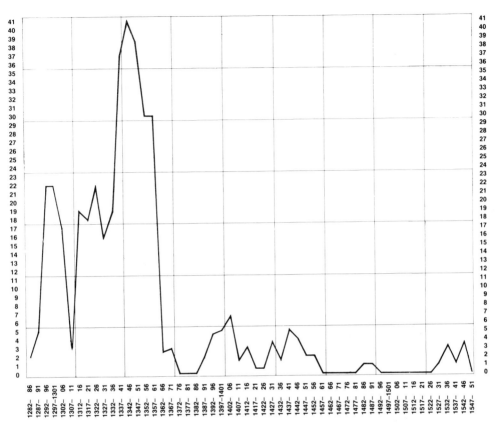

Graph showing the number of royal stud accounts in five-yearly periods.

Edward I came to the throne after a period of civil war which, as already mentioned, had probably disorganized and reduced the studs of both the King and his subjects. When his father died on 16 November 1272 Edward was away on crusade, and he did not return to England until August 1274. Just over two years later, in November 1276, he declared war on the Welsh. It was only then that he realized he was short of horses. Between 15 November 1276 and 7 February 1277 he imported 158 horses through Wissant and Dover, and gave various of his barons permission to import 45

87

more.[54] He would just have had time to send the better stallions on a visit to the studs before they assembled with the feudal host at Worcester on 24 July 1277. It was not until 1282, when the Second Welsh War was beginning, that he seems to have realized that planning was necessary if he was to maintain a large force of cavalry permanently. In that year he ordained that all those who held £30 worth of land should 'meet the scarcity of the great horses suitable for war, by procuring such a horse with appropriate horse-armour' and keep it ready for use.[55] This is the first use of the term 'great horse' (*magnus equus*) in the records, and it is particularly useful as it shows that at any rate in this instance it was applied to the ordinary cavalry horse (*competens ad arma*). It is in this year also that the *Equitia* accounts begin, and in the next year we find Edward building stables at Clipstone (Nottinghamshire) at a cost of £108.8s.5d.[56] Expenditure on the studs increased rapidly until 1301, after which the opposition of the clergy and barons, which had culminated in the Confirmation of the Charters in 1297, at last began to have an effect, and the King could be seen to be economizing.

Edward II (1307–27) revived the studs with the utmost vigour. Quite apart from the fact that he had the Scottish war on his hands, he and his favourite, Piers Gaveston, had an enthusiasm for horsebreeding very like that subsequently demonstrated by King Charles I and George Villiers, Duke of Buckingham. In 1305, two years before he came to the throne, Edward had bought the Earl of Warenne's stud at Ditchling in Sussex and written to the Archbishop of Canterbury (no less) to beg for the loan of a good stallion, besides commissioning a Lombard merchant, William Persona, to buy him horses and mares in Lombardy.[57] In 1309, two years after his accession, he sent his agents, the brothers Bynde and Philip Bonaventura, to Lombardy to buy twenty destriers and twelve mares – the mares being particularly significant because they would have been used only for breeding.[58] In 1313 he sent William de Toulouse to Spain for thirty destriers, some of which were subsequently described as 'great horses' (*equis magnis* or *equis magnis cursariis*). In 1314–15 William de Toulouse and his brother

37 Part of the account roll of Arnold Garcia (1332–3), detailing the horses he had bought for King Edward III in Spain. It begins with the purchase of 'unius dextrarii griselpomyle' (a dapple grey destrier) for £60.

Pons brought the King sixteen horses which they had purchased for £531, the cheapest, described as a grey flecked black (greys geste de more), costing £15, and the most expensive, a silver-grey warhorse (un destrier liard grys), £75.[59]

The deposition of Edward II (1327) and the consequential reforms caused an immediate fall in the number of *Equitia* accounts, but as soon as Edward III had shaken off his tutelage and commenced his personal rule in 1330, the activity of the stud department increased at an astonishing rate. At first the major purchases were from Spain, as in the previous reign. In 1332–3 Arnold Garcia bought nineteen horses there for the King at a cost of £649; this time the prices ranged from £10 to £60, with additional expenses of £66.11s. for travel, maintenance and gratuities.[60] But after 1342 imports from Spain dried up; this may have been due to reluctance on the part of the Castilians who had made an alliance with the French,[61] but alternatively it could have been because of a preference for the larger horses available from Lombardy, Flanders and Brabant. In addition to his own purchases,

37

38 The battle of Crécy, with bowmen as prominent as cavalry. From a fifteenth-century manuscript of Froissart's Chronicles.

Edward III often had to compensate his allies for the loss of horses which they had suffered. In 1341 he promised to compensate his brother-in-law, the Count of Hainault, to the tune of 25,000 Florentine florins (£3,958. 6s.8d.), for those lost two years before at the siege of Buironfosse.[62]

The peak years for the *Equitia* accounts were 1342–6, culminating with the battle of Crécy (1346). After that there was a decline which should probably be associated with the Black Death (1348–9) and the consequential shortage of labour and very sharp rise in wages and prices. The decline of the *Equitia* was checked in 1357–61, the years immediately after the battle of Poitiers (1346), but the royal studs were beginning to sell almost as many horses as they bought. In 1357 the King decided to sell all but the twelve best mares in his stud at Windsor in order to raise money for his new castle there, but he got no more than £6 for fourteen mares and thirteen fillies. Presumably the prices were low because the cost of feeding and stabling had risen so enormously that ordinary people were reluctant to encumber themselves with additional horses. In 1359 Edward III bought forty-eight horses from a Lombard merchant called Minello de Viterbo, and though we do not know the price, we do know that the cost of boarding them for ten days in the Black Prince's park at Kennington was £13.9s., or about $6\frac{3}{4}d.$ per horse per day: the hay cost 2d., the oats 3d., service 1d., and litter about $\frac{1}{2}d.$; lights and other incidentals accounted for the remaining farthing.[63]

In 1360 the Treaty of Brétigny heralded a decisive change in the *Equitia*. Though the peace lasted only nine years, it offered both the King and his subjects the opportunity to reflect on the relative cost and usefulness of warhorses. The English victories at Crécy and Poitiers had been won against the superior cavalry forces of the French, largely because of the power of the English bowmen, whose wages of 4d. a day were less than two-thirds of what it cost to board one warhorse for a day. It would have been strange if the King and his advisers had not drawn the conclusion that expenses could be reduced very greatly if fewer horses were maintained. In 1360 there were $7\frac{1}{2}$ rolls of *Equitia* accounts, in 1361 the equivalent of 2, and in 1362, 1365 and 1368 the equivalent of one each. In 1369 there were the equivalent of 3 rolls, but after that no more until 1387.

38

The maintenance of horses is always an expensive business. In the first place one needs somewhere to keep them, the obvious place being in parks. Before 1360 the most important parks for the king's horses in the division North of the Trent were Haverah, Little Park and Bilton in Knaresborough Forest (West Yorkshire), Burstwick (East Yorkshire), Ighton Hill Park (Lancashire) and Macclesfield Park (Cheshire). South of the Trent there were many more, those most frequently mentioned being at Windsor (Berkshire), Woodstock (Oxfordshire) and Guildford (Surrey). Others were at Risborough (i.e. Princes Risborough, Buckinghamshire) where the Black Prince had his stud, Odiham (Hampshire) Henly Park (Surrey), Tonbridge and Knole (Kent), Rayleigh and Writtle (Essex), Hadenham (Cambridgeshire), Cornbury and (North) Oseney (Oxfordshire), Hampstead Marshal and Stratfield Mortimer (Berkshire), Cippenham (in Burnham, Buckinghamshire) and Yardley Hastings (Northamptonshire). Not all of these were on land that was genuine royal demesne. Several of them (e.g. Burstwick, Yardley Hastings, North Oseney and Stratfield Mortimer) were in the hands of the Crown only because of escheat or wardship, and could be expected to pass into other hands quite soon. Considering those parks which appear only fleetingly in the accounts – Howden, Selby and Cave (East Yorkshire), Hargrave in Arden and Solihull (Warwickshire), Horsington (Somerset) and Sonning (Berkshire) – one gets the impression that whenever there was a secular wardship or ecclesiastical vacancy, the king's agents moved in quickly to see if it included a park which could be 'depastured' by the king's horses before the new heir was installed. Depasturing results when horses are left for too long a period in the same pasture; since they will not eat the grass which grows up around their own droppings, the field eventually becomes a mass of unpalatable tufts of coarse grass. It was this that Sir John Brocas was complaining about in 1363 when he declared that the park at Guildford was no longer profitable because it had been 'depastured' by the King's mares and fillies over the previous twelve years.[64]

It is never possible to feed horses on grass alone. Additional fodder is required. The king's horses in the fourteenth century required enormous quantities of hay, oats, beans and pease. If purchased on the open market, this could be very expensive, so the king usually instructed his sheriffs to obtain what was required by 'buying and purveying', which meant that the purchase price was fixed not by bargaining but by the purveyor's order. The purveyor's prices were always on the low side, but in the 1350s they tended to be extremely low because the purveyors, as officials of the king, would insist on complying with the Statute of Labourers which attempted to fix both prices and wages without reference to the rapid inflation which occurred after the Black Death. Consequently the king's horses were not only expensive but also unpopular. No one wanted them to be quartered in their county.

A further difficulty was the murrain. During the first half of the fourteenth century the country was overcrowded with horses, for it was not only the king who was breeding them but also very many of his subjects, and as a result the risk of infectious sickness or murrain was increased. It is not always easy to detect how frequent or severe the incidence of murrain really was, because it is recorded at different times in different ways. In one roll covering the period 1317–24 John de Redmere, keeper of the horses South of the Trent, recorded murrain only because the hides of the dead horses had been sold. The parks concerned were at Windsor, Woodstock, Rayleigh, Cornbury, Princes Risborough and Odiham, and the total deaths for the seven years were 7 stallions (2 of them destriers), one 'horse', 82 mares and 163 foals and fillies, the park worst affected (or infected) being Woodstock which accounted for 4 of the stallions, one destrier, 29 mares and 71 foals or fillies.[65] In another roll, this time of 1357–8, Sir John Brocas listed the deaths of 12 mares, 4 colts and 11 fillies at Dorchester, Yardley Hastings and Guildford, simply in order to exonerate their keeper of carelessness.[66] The Black Death does not seem to have spread to the king's horses at all.

Nonetheless, changed military and economic circumstances and the complaints of the king's subjects all militated in favour of a reduction in the number of royal studs. The receipts from selling off the horses may have been small, but the saving in wages was very considerable. Until 1361 it had been necessary to organize the studs in two separate divisions, North and South of the Trent. The heads or keepers of these divisions had been:

NORTH OF THE TRENT

John de Newsham (*Neusom*), 1322–36
Edmund de Tidmarsh (*Thedmershe*), 1336–42
Roger de Normanville, 1342–50
John de Barton, 1350–57
Thomas de Botha, 1358–61

William de Beauxamys, 1311–16
(in fact, though without the title)
Brother John de Redmere, 1317–25
(in fact, though without the title, and perhaps beyond 1325)
Arnold Garcia, 1330–39 (see p. 89)
Menald Brocas, 1341–4
William de Fremelsworth, 1344–61
who had under him two successive 'keepers of the great
horses in the South', viz. William le Ferrour ('the smith'),
1344–54, and Edmund Rose, 1354–60

One cannot always be certain of the wages of these men. In
1315–16 William de Beauxamys received 12*d.* a day, which put
him on the same level as the king's chief master-mason, but in 1354
William de Fremelsworth was receiving only 3*d.* a day. In 1354
Edmund Rose (keeper of the great horses) was receiving 3*d.* a day
also, but in 1359 his wage had risen to 3½*d.* a day. At the same time
(1359) Thomas de Botha, keeper in the North, was receiving 8*d.* a
day and 20*s.* for his robe, while all his subordinates received 2*d.* a
day and 10*s.* for their robes.[67] The most probable explanation for
the variations in the wages of the chief keepers is that they received
'usual fees' as well.

After 1361 the keeperships North and South of the Trent
disappear, and in their place we find an officer of knightly rank or

39 *A drawing of the tomb of Sir Bernard
Brocas (d. 1395) in Westminster Abbey.
He was the first Master of the Horse to be
buried there.*

military reputation, ultimately to be known as 'Master of the Horse'. The first man to have this position (though without the title) was probably Sir John Brocas, whose accounts we have already mentioned. He came from a minor family in Aquitaine and was probably a cousin of Menald Brocas (keeper of the studs South of the Trent, 1341–4). He had been active in the royal studs from 1330, not as a paid servant but as some sort of officer, though he is given no specific title. Horses are delivered to him or are despatched by him, he is styled 'lord' (*dominus*), and in general he appears in the same sort of context as had Piers Gaveston under Edward II.[68] In all respects he acted as if he were Master of the Horse in name, and it is probably significant that he was also chief forester of Windsor, Warden of Nottingham Gaol, and Constable of the town, castle and park of Guildford. He died in 1365 and was succeeded by his son Bernard (named after his paternal uncle who had made the family fortune as a royal clerk and established the family's seat of Beaurepaire in Hampshire). The younger Bernard was in charge of the king's horses for a short while, but like his father had no specific title. He moved on to higher and better things when he was appointed Captain of Calais.[69] By 1383 we find Sir Thomas Moreaux (or Morieux or Murreaux) not only in charge of the king's horses but officially styled 'Master of the Horse'.[70] As so often happens, a post that had ceased to be onerous had become honorific. Subsequent holders of the office up to 1509 were:[71]

39

1 Sir Thomas de Clifford, before 1388
2 Sir John Russell, 1390–97
3 Sir Richard Redman, 1397–9
4 Robert de Waterton, 1399–1416
5 John de Waterton, 1416–20
6 Sir Henry Noon, 1420–28
7 Richard Beauchamp, Earl of Warwick, 1428–9
8 Sir Walter de Beauchamp, 1429–30
9 Sir John Styward, 1430–40
10 John Lord Beauchamp of Powyck, 1440–57/8
11 Sir Thomas de Burgh, Lord of Gainsborough, 1465–75

12 Sir John Cheyne, 1475–83
13 Sir Thomas Tyrrell, 1483
14 Sir James Tyrrell (brother of Thomas), 1483–5
15 Sir Thomas Brandon, 1485–1509

In the period of the Masters of the Horse the *Equitia* accounts are only a fraction of what they had been before. Reference to the graph on p. 87 will show that in the last nine years of Richard II's reign (1377–99) and the first half of Henry IV's (1399–1413) there was an increase of activity which, though trivial compared with that of the first half of the century, must have seemed significant at the time. Henry IV's parliaments did not grant him money easily, and it is not surprising that the *Equitia* accounts declined in the second half of his reign. Henry V (1413–22) secured a modest revival for his Agincourt campaign (1415) and slightly larger revivals coincide with the siege of Orleans (1428–9) and Talbot's campaigns in Normandy (1437–43). The Hundred Years War, of which these campaigns were a part, came to an end in 1453, but by then civil war (the Wars of the Roses) had broken out in England. There are no *Equitia* accounts between 1459 and 1480, and though this complete blank may be due to some administrative accident, it is not difficult to see that the disturbed conditions would have made it difficult for anyone, king or noble, to maintain his studs in perfect order. The changes of king as the fortunes of war fluctuated, forfeitures, and the passage of hostile armies, must all have been responsible for the breakdown of many studs and the sale of many others in order to raise money for ransoms. The greatest demand for warhorses came from Italy where, much to the amazement of intelligent observers like Machiavelli, princes and cities still believed a large force of cavalry was essential for a successful army. Knights from other countries, particularly England and France, migrated to Italy with private armies, hiring themselves out as *condottieri* to various city states. One of the earlier ones was Sir John
40 Hawkwood (d. 1394), celebrated for the fresco of him painted in 1436 by Paolo Uccello in the form of an equestrian monument in Florence Cathedral.

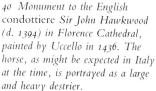

40 *Monument to the English* condottiere *Sir John Hawkwood (d. 1394) in Florence Cathedral, painted by Uccello in 1436. The horse, as might be expected in Italy at the time, is portrayed as a large and heavy destrier.*

That, at any rate, was the impression which the Tudors liked to give. Just as they blamed their predecessors for the weakness of royal government and the growth of over-mighty subjects, so they declared that their own shortage of cavalry horses, or indeed of any good horses at all, was due to the fact that too many had been sold abroad. King Henry VII prohibited their export in 1495[72] and in the next century his son, Henry VIII, was to embark on a considerable policy for the revival of horsebreeding in England. But before we can understand the full significance of what he did, we must turn to examine developments that occurred in Italy, for Henry VIII prided himself on being a Renaissance prince, and realized that even in matters of war and warhorses the new courtly fashions were important.

5

The Impact of the Renaissance: Veterinary Medicine and Equestrianism

Although this book is about the 'medieval' warhorse, it cannot stop short of the Renaissance just because the Renaissance is deemed to be part of Modern History. Having seen how, by the use of selective breeding, men were able to design and produce a warhorse according to their own specifications, it is only natural to ask how and why they became sufficiently dissatisfied with the result to design and produce a different sort of horse. The fact that this second design was realized in a period which historians call the Renaissance is no reason for refusing to follow our equine theme to the logical conclusion. Neither the 'Middle Ages' nor the 'Renaissance' are objective realities. They are useful concepts only so long as they are not treated as watertight compartments. For historians of science the modern world begins not with the fifteenth or sixteenth century but with the scientific revolution of the seventeenth century. Similarly the historian of horses finds the great divide at the point where one dominant type, the medieval warhorse or destrier, is replaced by another, the English Thoroughbred.

It must also be stated that no book on medieval history can exclude the Renaissance entirely, for though the English like to think of the Renaissance as beginning with the Tudors in 1485, many European historians trace its origins to the thirteenth century. That was when Greek was first studied in the schools of Western Europe, when the first great advances were made in painting by Giotto (1267–1337), in literature by Dante (1256–1321) and in experimental science by Roger Bacon (1214–93). It is true that some of these promising beginnings were in danger of stagnating in the fourteenth century, but nonetheless they were real, as can be seen in the two aspects of the Renaissance which

41 Henry VIII arriving on his white Neapolitan, before the meeting at the Field of Cloth of Gold (1520). 'No animal is more noble than the horse,' observed the thirteenth-century Italian 'vet' Jordanus Ruffus, 'since it is by horses that princes, magnates and knights are separated from lesser people and because a lord cannot fittingly be seen among private citizens except through the mediation of a horse.'

concerned horses most directly – the great advances made in veterinary medicine and surgery, and the rediscovery of Xenophon's short but powerful tract *Hippike* (On Horsemanship).

VETERINARY MEDICINE

The advances in veterinary medicine are first observable in the 1250s. Previously the standard work on the subject was the *Hippiatria* (Horse-medicine), a Byzantine work compiled in the reign of Constantine VII Porphyrogenitos (944–59) from a variety of treatises of the fourth and fifth centuries AD including the *Mulomedicina* (Horse-medicine) of Chiron 'the Centaur' and Apsyrtos of Prusa, and others by a veterinary surgeon called 'Hierocles' and a mysterious 'Hippocrates'.[1] It was natural that this obscure Hippocrates should be confused with the great physician of Cos who lived in the fifth century BC, and the confusion lent authority to a number of statements which otherwise might have been treated with scepticism. The great point to grasp, however, is that the *Hippiatria*, though written in Greek, was composed in the late Antique period and was not representative of the science of classical Greece. Like the curate's egg it was good in parts, with many practical remedies which had been discovered empirically, but little scientific understanding. It had been translated from the Greek into Arabic, and by the thirteenth century into Latin (probably from the Arabic) in Sicily or South Italy.

An alternative book of horse-medicine which was in circulation even earlier was the *Mulomedicina* of Vegetius (Flavius Vegetius Renatus) who flourished in the last twenty years of the fourth century AD. The fact that this was a relatively ancient Latin text seems to have given it respectability, but in fact it was very like the *Hippiatria*, being based on a Latin translation of one of its main sources, the *Mulomedicina* of Chiron 'the Centaur' and Apsyrtos of Prusa.

The learned, particularly those who had had a university education, preferred Aristotle's treatise on animals (*De Animalibus* or *Historia Animalium*), which was known in Latin translation at any rate by 1210. This book, 'an introductory collection of facts about animal life', contains a certain amount of accurate observation, with a brief account of some twenty-five illnesses which might affect horses. So far as it went, it had many virtues, but since it was written by Aristotle, scholars studied it not as part of science or medicine but as something on its own, and commented on it almost as if it had been the Word of God.

This was the great weakness of medieval academics, but it was recognized and attacked by a few rare spirits at a surprisingly early date. The earliest of them, Adelard of Bath, left the schools of Laon in Northern France in the first quarter of the twelfth century in order to study with the Arabs, perhaps at Salerno in South Italy, where Arabic medicine had already been introduced by Constantinus Africanus. Explaining his position to a nephew left at Laon, Adelard wrote: 'It is difficult for me to discuss the nature of animals with you, because I learnt from my masters the Arabs to follow the light of reason, while you are led by the bridle of authority; for what other word than "bridle" can I use to describe authority?'[2]

A century later similar sentiments were expressed by the Emperor Frederick II (1212–50). He also knew about Arabic learning, because he had been brought up in Sicily. In his book *De Arte venandi cum Avibus* (On the Art of Hunting with Birds) he stated that it was his purpose to put aside the teaching of Aristotle who was 'ignorant of the practice of falconry', and to record instead what he had learnt by observation and practice: 'In his [Aristotle's] work, the *Liber Animalium*, we find many quotations from other authors whose statements he did not verify and who, in their turn, were not speaking from experience. Entire conviction of the truth never follows from mere hearsay.'[3] What Frederick wanted to do was to describe things 'as they were', and he fired his followers with a determination to do the same. His knight-farrier, Jordanus Ruffus (Giordano Ruffo) of Calabria, wrote *De Medicina Equorum* (On the Medicine of Horses), a book which owed nothing to the *Hippiatria*, Vegetius or Aristotle but was the original work of a practising veterinary surgeon, based on his own observations. A modern vet has described him as a 'consummate practitioner' and hailed his work as 'the starting point of all the treatises of animal pathology'.[4] Unfortunately, though the title which Jordanus gave his book was specific, his nineteenth-century editor chose to rename it *Hippiatria*, apparently in the belief that this was the only medieval word for horse-medicine, and unaware that it denoted the very sort of compilation which Jordanus would have denounced as ignorant.[5]

Jordanus was not a humble farrier. He styled himself *miles in marestala* (which I have rendered 'knight-farrier', though 'knight in the marshalcy' might be more literal if less comprehensible) and came of a noble family, his uncle, Petrus Ruffus, being Grand Marshal of the Kingdom and governor of Calabria and Sicily, while he himself was justiciar or castellan of Montecassino and Pontecorvo, in addition to his appointment in the 'marshalcy'. He wrote his book after Frederick II's death (1250), and probably before 1256 when, in the midst of civil war, he was captured by enemies who put his eyes out.[6]

At the beginning he states that it was not his purpose to compile a compendium of everything known about horses, but to write down those things which he had observed himself: 'But as God has shown me, I will set out in order what has been put to the test by me, Jordanus Ruffus of Calabria, *miles in marestala* of the late lord Emperor Frederick II, to the reverence of whose most sacred memory I will most diligently adhere by showing real reasons for everything.'[7] The main part of his book is concerned with the diseases and wounds of horses and the best methods of treating them, but he prefaces it with short chapters on how horses are bred and born, how captured, tamed, kept and trained, and how their points are to be judged. So far as breeding is concerned, Jordanus considered it important that a stallion put to stud should be well cared for and ridden little, if at all; that pregnant mares should not be shut up by day or night, lest they suffer from hunger or thirst; that foals should be born at a season when there was plenty of grass, and preferably in a district which was steep and stony, so that they would get rough exercise from the day of their birth, thus toughening their hooves and strengthening their legs; and finally that foals should run with their dams for two years (presumably he did not expect his mares to foal more frequently than every other year), but in the third be removed and kept apart from the fillies and mares, so as to build up their strength with plenty of free exercise, good pasture and immunity from the accidents attendant on sexual exertions.[8]

In his main text Jordanus describes sixty-five different diseases or injuries and their remedies. They include glanders, angina, bad wind, retention of urine, swelling of the testicles, enteritis, ailments of the eyes, mouth and tongue, lesions on all parts of the body, grape, fistulae and horse-pox. He writes simply and concisely and experts are united in his praise. Though he is not always correct in his diagnoses and remedies, his book marks a decisive advance in veterinary medicine because of its use of scientific observation, establishing a sound basis for the development of animal pathology. In the Mediterranean world its value was recognized rapidly, and it remained in use throughout the Middle Ages. It has been preserved in forty-one medieval manuscripts, eighteen of them in Latin (the language in which it was originally written), thirteen in Italian, three in Sicilian, four in French, one in Provençal and two in Catalan. The Italian text was printed in Venice in 1492, and four more editions were printed there or at Bologna by 1563.[9]

An early successor to Jordanus was Teodorico Borgognoni, a Dominican friar who died in 1298. Very much an all-rounder, he wrote a book on surgery c. 1267, as well as two veterinary works, one of them on hawks, the other on horses. He states that he learnt his medicine from Hugo of Lucca (d. 1252) whom the Bolognese had retained as a surgeon for their army, and he calls him his 'father', probably in the sense of 'master'. As a Dominican, Teodorico could be expected to have book-learning, and it has been shown that the two principal sources for his work on horses were the *Mulomedicina* of Vegetius and *De Medicina Equorum* of Jordanus Ruffus. His originality (though it may have been that of his 'father') lay in his insistence on cleaning wounds thoroughly, so as to remove all foreign bodies from them before they were sewn up, combined with his recipes for putting patients (whether human or equine) to sleep before operating on them. As a friar he was committed to a more or less itinerant life and to the vow of poverty, but in view of his exceptional work he was given as a sinecure the bishopric of Cervia on the Adriatic coast of North Italy. His book on horse-medicine must have been written within twenty years of that of Jordanus Ruffus, an impressive indication of the rapidity with which Jordanus's text had become known. It is also interesting, but not surprising, that Teodorico, who would already have been in his sixties, was not prepared to jettison Vegetius's work completely, but preferred to use it in harness, as it were, with the new work from the south. Teodorico's work did not have so wide a circulation as that of Jordanus; it survives in twelve manuscripts, nine of them in Latin and three in Provençal.[10] It did, however, serve as one of the main sources for the *Libro de los Caballos* (Horse Book) which was written by an unknown author at the court of Alfonso X of Castile and Leon (1252–84) and helped to spread the new teaching in Spain: five manuscripts of this text are known in Castilian, and three in Catalan.[11]

The further north one goes in Europe, the smaller are the signs of any serious interest in veterinary science. There is one manuscript, now in Paris, of a work entitled *Libro de Menescalcia de Albeyteria et Fisica de las Bestias* (Book of the Marshal, Vet and Animal-medicine) which was written in Catalan by Johan Alvares de Salamiellas at the request of 'Johan de Béarn, knight, steward of Bigorre and captain of Lourdes, for Our Lord the King of England and France'. The king must have been Edward III (1327–77), but whether he ever saw the book is doubtful. In any case, though it makes some use of Teodorico's work, it makes notably greater use of the veterinary Hippocrates and other parts of the Byzantine *Hippiatria*.[12]

The most important follower of Jordanus Ruffus was Laurentius Rusius (Lorenzo Rusio), whose *Liber de Marescalcia* or *Mascalcia* (Book of Marshalcy) was dedicated to Cardinal Napoleone Orsini and must therefore have been written between 1288 and 1342. In his dedicatory letter Laurentius styles himself 'marshal of the city of Rome' (*mariscalcus de urbe*); clearly this is one of the cases where

42

42 *A horse suspended in slings while its leg is treated, from the* Libro de Menescalcia de Albeyteria et Fisica de las Bestias *of Johan Alvares de Salamiellas.*

'marshal' means 'horse-doctor' (cf. pp. 84–5), but we are left guessing whether this designation indicated a public office, or was just a way of saying that he was a horse-doctor practising in Rome. He says that he had studied horse-medicine since he was a boy, benefiting from the fact that 'marshals' came to Rome from all over the world. He admits also to having studied books, naming 'Magister Maurus' and the veterinary Hippocrates, names which denoted different versions of the Byzantine *Hippiatria*, but his greatest debt was to Jordanus Ruffus, whose 76 chapters he rearranged but reproduced entire, with the addition of a few stylistic flourishes. Laurentius also made an original contribution of his own. His book is more than twice the length of Jordanus's, having 181 chapters, with much new material apparently stemming from his own experience. It is a pity that it cannot be dated within limits narrower than 1288–1342, because it marks the point at which Jordanus's work was not only accepted as an authority but also used as a springboard for further advances. The circulation of Laurentius's book almost rivalled that of Jordanus's, with eighteen manuscripts extant, thirteen of them in Latin, three in Italian and one each in French and Flemish, together with eleven printed editions by 1563.[13] Indirectly much of his work also reached Spain. When Alfonso V of Aragon conquered Naples in 1443 his major-domo, Manuel Díaz of Calatayud, came across the work of Laurentius Rusius for the first time. He made considerable use of it, together with the *Libro de los Caballos* with which he was already acquainted, in a work of his own, the *Libro de Albeyteria* (Vet's Book), which had a good circulation in Spain with eleven extant manuscripts in Catalan and eight printed editions in Castilian.[14]

An interesting view of veterinary medicine in fourteenth-century Florence is given by Dino Dini, who wrote his *Mascalcia* (Marshalcy) in that city, as he himself tells us, between 19 January 1352 and 29 December 1359 – that is to say in the decade after the Black Death. In many respects his book is a disappointment, for one might have expected that a Florentine's work would have been marked by new scientific observations. But Dino Dini seems to have had a chip on his shoulder. He came of a family of marshals – he says he was the seventh practising marshal in three generations – but had originally hoped to better himself. Most marshals, he said, were the sons of labourers, brought up rustically with the rough-and-ready knowledge of herdsmen. He admitted a few exceptions: Minuccio, the marshal of Guido, Bishop of Arezzo, who was not only skilled in his craft but also 'a fine speaker, very cultivated and well-mannered'; Pietro from Cortona who could castrate a standing horse; and Andrea, a splendid marshal who knew the text of Vegetius's *Mulomedicina* by heart, so that whenever he saw a sick horse he knew which chapter to refer to. So far as veterinary matters were concerned, Dino based himself on the *Hippiatria* and the works of Vegetius, Jordanus Ruffus and Teodorico Borgognoni. In other words, he was reasonably up-to-date, but had nothing much to contribute himself. He wrote in Italian, presumably in the hope of a wide readership, but only three manuscripts of his work are known.[15]

As already suggested, the circulation of books on veterinary medicine was virtually confined to the lands bordering the Western Mediterranean. South Italy, if one includes Rome in it, was responsible for almost all the important advances, with Aragon and Castile in second place. A certain amount of interest in the subject was shown in North Italy, though it contributed little that was original, perhaps because the superior status of those who practised medicine on humans depressed the status of vets.

Most remarkable, however, is the apparent indifference of the kingdoms of France and England, the most renowned centres of chivalry, to the development of veterinary science. We have seen that one copy of a Spanish work was destined for Edward III of England, but the only original work to have been compiled in North-West Europe was that of Guillaume de Villiers, known as the 'pretender' of Gonneville (one of several places of that name in Normandy). He gave his book no title, and neither his status nor his dates are known, though one of the three surviving manuscripts is dated 1456. His principal source was Jordanus Ruffus, but he also used the *Hippiatria*, probably through the work of Teodorico Borgognoni. His original contributions concern infections of the eyes, together with a variety of magic charms.[16]

THE IMPACT OF THE RENAISSANCE IN ENGLAND

So far as can be seen, none of these veterinary works reached England in any shape or form before the sixteenth century. Yvonne Poulle-Drieux, who is the authority on them, has pointed out the fact with astonishment, but in truth it is only one example of the slowness with which the English accepted the ideas of the Italian Renaissance in any of its manifestations. It was only under the Tudors that the English began to realize that their cultural isolation could prove a disadvantage.

This fact is illustrated by an observation which some people might regard as trivial, although in most periods of history it has been important. To a large extent kings and princes were judged by their appearance, and that in turn was often determined by their horses. Jordanus Ruffus himself had made the point when he wrote: 'No animal is more noble than the horse, since it is by horses that princes, magnates and knights are separated from lesser people and because a lord cannot fittingly be seen among private citizens except through the mediation of a horse.'[17] From a horse a prince could look down on his subjects, move through them without being jostled, and hear their complaints without losing his freedom to move on. But obviously the image projected depended on the horse as much as the rider. For normal occasions a palfrey would be what was required, though it needed to be particularly fine. But now the courts of Renaissance Europe were specializing in what could be described as the 'courtly' horse, which was as beautiful as it was practical. Fully trained for the manoeuvres of battle, it could be used for both display and jousting. Such horses could not be found in England.

For King Henry VIII that was a serious matter. He was very anxious to be a Renaissance prince, and in that spirit made arrangements for a spectacular meeting with King Francis I of France at the Field of Cloth of Gold in 1520. Naturally he had to have suitable mounts. His diplomats and agents were told to be on the look-out for them everywhere in Europe, but particularly in Italy. From the Duke of Mantua (see pp. 112–13) he acquired a Frieslander bay, from the Duke of Ferrara a fine horse of the breed of Isabella, Duchess of Milan, and from the Emperor Charles V twenty-five beautiful Spanish horses. In the event the horse which he rode for the actual meeting came from Naples, while that of Francis I, who had been equally busy, was from Mantua.[18]

Henry VIII had suffered from a shortage of horses for his military exploits almost from the beginning of his reign.[19] As we have already seen (p. 97), his father thought that all the best horses had been sold abroad in the fifteenth century, and had prohibited further exports. But the situation remained serious, and Henry VIII came to the conclusion that more positive measures were required, and promoted three Acts of Parliament to increase the supply of horses. In an 'Acte concernyng the breeds of Horses' (1535), made necessary by 'the great decay of the generation and bredyng of good swyfte and strong Horses which here to fore have been bredde in this Realme', he ordained that every owner of an enclosed park should keep in it 'two Mares being not spayed apte and able to beare foles, each of them of the hieght of xiii handfulles at the lest'. In 1540 a further Act named thirty shires and districts in which no person was allowed to put in any forest, chase, moor, heath, common or waste where mares or fillies were kept, any stoned horse (i.e. stallion) over the age of two which was less than 15 hands high.[20] This Act (from which the term 'shire horse' for a large and heavy horse is derived) must have been difficult to enforce, but even if enforced strictly it would have marked a serious retreat from the organization of the fourteenth-century studs, back to a happy-go-lucky system, more or less in line with what we have described as Stage 1 in the development of horsebreeding (pp. 38–9).

Henry's third Act (1541–2) was more promising. It enjoined archbishops and dukes to maintain seven trotting horses for the saddle, each of them at least three years old and 14 hands high. Marquises, earls and bishops with incomes of £1,000 or above had to maintain five such horses, viscounts and barons with incomes of 1,000 marks three, and those with incomes of 500 marks two. Finally, one such horse had to be maintained by anyone in receipt of £100 a year 'whose wife shall wear any gown of silk, or . . . any French hood or bonnet of velvet, with any habiliment, paste, or egg of gold, pearl or stone, or any chain of gold about their neck or in their partlets, or in any apparel of their body'.[21] The cleverness of this Act was the formal way in which it equated social status and wealth with the number of saddle-horses maintained. It was an appeal to snobbery which was likely to be successful not only in producing the required number of horses, but also in encouraging an improvement in quality.

About this time Henry also established a body of Gentlemen Pensioners (fifty of them), who were members of the royal household required to provide horses for ceremonial and military occasions.[22] This meant that they had to keep studs, and to make this possible the King gave many of them parks which before the Dissolution (1536–9) had belonged to the monasteries. Thus Sir Francis Knollys received Caversham manor and park in Berkshire which previously had belonged to Reading Abbey and Ralph Fane parks round Tonbridge in Kent, one of which had previously belonged to the Knights of St John. Sir Nicholas Arnold (d. 1580) was given a park at Highnam which previously had belonged to Gloucester. He imported horses from Flanders, kept a fine stud of Neapolitan warhorses, and is reputed to have written a book on horsebreeding which, if ever it could be found, might prove to be the earliest in England. Other Gentlemen Pensioners who wrote books on the breeding and management of horses were Thomas Blundeville (c. 1560 etc.), Blundeville's friend Sir John Astley (1584), Thomas Bedingfield (1584) and Gervase Markham (1593). As we shall see, they were all much influenced by the doctrines of Italian horsemanship. To encourage them Henry VIII employed Italians as officers in his stables, Alexander de Bologna and Jacques de Granado in 1526 and 1544, Mathew de Mantua who was studman in 1545, and Master Hannibal the farrier. Others were to follow under Queen Elizabeth.

Ultimately the book which had most influence on men's attitude to horses was Xenophon's treatise, *Hippike* (On Horse-manship). The fact that it was one of the products of classical Greece ensured that it would be treated with respect: there were manuscripts of it in Italy (two of the thirteenth century are known, and five of the fourteenth), several references to it in the fifteenth century, an edition of it printed at Florence in 1516, and a Latin translation published in 1539.[23] It is short – about thirty-three pages of print – and though it does not give sufficient details to be a comprehensive handbook, it conveys very clearly, attractively and persuasively the idea that horses are best trained by kindness. Xenophon insisted that the first duty of an owner was to cherish his colt, so that it became fond of men. 'The one best rule and practice in dealing with a horse is never to approach him in anger' (vi, 13). When the colt is being trained to get used to crowds and the noises of the street, he may well shy at some things, but the man 'must teach him by quieting him and without impatience, that there is nothing to be afraid of' (ii, 6). In general, Xenophon concluded 'what a horse does under constraint . . . he does without understanding and with no more grace than a dancer would show if he was whipped and goaded' (xi, 6). This was the message which was taken up by the leaders of the new Italian horsemanship , and the way in which they expressed themselves shows that they considered their attitude to be revolutionary.

The most famous of these Italians was Federigo Grisone, gentleman of Naples, whom his contemporaries hailed as a new Xenophon. In his book *Gli Ordini di Cavalcare* (The Rules of Horsemanship), which was published at Naples in 1550, Grisone wrote that there were three essentials to be learnt by anyone aspiring to be a perfect horseman:

43

> First, to knowe how and when to helpe your Horse.
> Secondlie, how and when to correct him. And thirdlie, how and when to cherish him, and to make much of him.[24]

Grisone himself did not expect his teaching to be received by most people of his time

> because it appeareth unto them that this manner of teaching should be false and untrue, being verie straunge and out of use, from all other which were and be now in the world. But all they which hereafter shall see what good effects doo grow by this order of teaching, shall know the great goodness of the infinite grace that heaven dooth now yeeld them.[25]

Sum Humfredi Lloyd

GLI ORDINI
DI CAVALCARE
DI FEDERIGO GRISONE,
Gentil'huomo Napoletano.

CON *gratia et motu proprio di Papa Giulio Terzo:*
Et con *priuileggio dell'Illuftriff.* Vece Rè di
Napoli, *che per Anni Dieci nõ fi deba
biano ftampare: ù ftampan in
altri luoghi, non fi poſa
fano uendere.*
A N N O *Domini*, M. D. L.

Lumley

43 *Title page of Grisone's* Gli Ordini di Cavalcare, *stating that it was published with the favour, and at the suggestion, of Pope Julius III (who was the patron also of Michelangelo, Palestrina and the bibliophile Marcello Cervini). This particular copy of the book was acquired by the great Welsh antiquary Humphrey Lloyd (1527–68) for the library of his brother-in-law John Baron Lumley (d. 1609) at Lumley Castle, Co. Durham. On the Baron's death the library was bought by Henry, Prince of Wales, like Lumley a connoisseur of horses (see Ill. 49).*

In fact Grisone was mistaken; his book was an enormous success. Though it did not appeal to the old-fashioned who wanted horses which were above all heavy and strong enough to meet any opposition with unstoppable force, it appealed greatly to those who thought it more important for a warhorse to be agile and obedient, trained to perform intricate manoeuvres, or to execute a *croupade*, jumping off the ground and kicking in mid-air, or a *capriole*, rising up on the back legs. The controversy as to which sort of horse was best lasted throughout the sixteenth century and well into the seventeenth; it will be recalled (p. 29) that in 1658 William Cavendish, himself a strong advocate of the new type of horse, thought it necessary to address himself briefly to those who still held the contrary opinion. For most of this period tilting remained a popular sport for aristocrats (King Henry II of France died of wounds received in the tilt in 1559), and for such occasions full armour was worn. It was the old-fashioned who wanted heavy horses and armour in real battles. Those who fought professionally saw the advantages to be gained from the agility of the new type of horse in combat, but a twelfth-century knight would have been horrified if he could have seen General Fairfax at the battle of Naseby (1645) mounted on a grey mare.

Grisone commended his practice of riding not only to the military, for whom he thought it very necessary, but also the courtly classes who had been educated to revere culture as expressed by the writers of the ancient world. If they had not actually read Xenophon, they would at least have been told about him; and because Xenophon's treatise *On Horsemanship* was not a book of detailed instructions but a simple thesis, its message could be conveyed by word of mouth. How well it fitted with the courtly

44   beliefs can be seen in the famous Hall of Horses in the Palazzo del Té at Mantua. Federigo Gonzaga, the first duke, had it painted in 1527–8 with portraits of his favourite horses. Since his stud was one of the most famous in Europe, the horses portrayed can be taken as a fair sample of the ideal at which the whole courtly class was aiming. The predominant blood in their make-up seems to have been Barb.

The central ideas of the courtly horse and equestrianism were well received by the upper classes in England, the essential books being translated and circulated quite rapidly. The first translation of Grisone's book of 1550 was *The Art of Riding* by Thomas Blundeville, which is undated but must have been published between 1559 and 1564, since it is dedicated to Robert Dudley as Master of the Horse and Knight of the Garter, but not as Earl of Leicester. As Blundeville himself put it, he began by translating Grisone literally, but finding that unsatisfactory put it in better form so that it was 'the playner and also the briefer'. The key word which he had to explain was 'management', a word not previously known in England. It was derived from the Latin *manus*, a hand, and meant (at this date) the handling or training of horses.

This Italian word *maneggiare*, is as much to say in English, as to handle with skil, as when we say, he can handle his Horse

44 *The Hall of Horses in the Palazzo del Tè, painted for Federigo II Gonzaga, the first Duke of Mantua, in 1527–8 by subordinates of Giulio Romano. The one who executed the portraits of the Duke's favourite horses is thought to have been Rinaldo Mantovano, who specialized in animals.*

or Weapon verie well: and amongst the *Italians* it is taken as a generall word, comprehending foure especiall kinds of maneging: whereof one is, when they make their Horse to double his turnes, which they call *Raddopiare*: an other is, when they make him to gallop the field, going in and out, as they do in skirmish: the third is, when they make him to leape aloft, and to fetch diuerse faults: the fourth is, when they pace, trot, or gallop him a good while to and fro, in one selfe path, the length of xx or xxx paces, or there about, turning him at ech and therof, either with single turne, whole turne, or double turne: which *Grison* calleth, *Maneggiare a Repoloni*. But we English men doe onelie call this last kind a manege, and that absolutelie without anie other addition.[26]

Robert Dudley, Earl of Leicester, while he was Queen Elizabeth's Master of the Horse (1558–81), brought a well known Italian horseman, Claudio Corte of Pavia, to England and made him his riding-master in 1565. Since Claudio published a book on horsemanship (*Il Cavalarizzo*) in 1573, we know something about his methods. In his preface he refers to earlier writers, including Aristotle and Pliny, but declares repeatedly that the best by far was Xenophon, and like him he desired 'that above all horses should be taught gently and with great patience'. He gives plans of the rings which should be laid out for the exercising of horses and explains the benefits of his system.

Touching the profit which proceedeth from trotting the rings, I saie that it bringeth the horse to be well-breathed, it maketh his shoulders and legges nimble, it settleth his head and necke, it maketh him to beare light on the hand, it giueth him heart and courage, it maketh him willing to turne on either hande indifferentlie, it correcteth all evill conditions, and the horsse becomes more apt and disposed to the shorte turnes, and euerie other kind of manage.

The use of the ring is necessarie for skirmish, for battell, and for combate, either offending or defending. It is also a comelie sight in the rider, and standeth him in steed for the exercise of the turneie, and all other feates of armes.

Moreover, it is a thing that naturallie horses doo loue: which is prooued, in that young foles, so soone as they are borne, doo presentlie runne about, plaieng as it were in circular wise. I doo therefore conclude that the ring turnes are things of much importance.[27]

The translation is by Sir Thomas Bedingfield, whose *Art of Riding according to Claudio Corte* was published in London in 1584, only eleven years after the Italian edition. He was one of the Queen's Gentlemen Pensioners (above, pp. 109–10), but he was not alone in his enthusiasm. Some gentlemen built 'riding houses' in their own grounds. Few of these have survived, but at Wolfeton House in Charminster (Dorset) one which was probably built by Sir George Trenchard, in the last quarter of the sixteenth century, has been identified and studied in detail.[28]   45

Another Italian who came to England, this time at the invitation of Sir Philip Sidney, was Prospero d'Osma. He established a riding school at Mile End outside London, and in 1576 the Earl of Leicester, as Master of the Horse, commissioned him to report on the royal studs at Malmesbury (Wiltshire) and Tutbury (Staffordshire). His general conclusion was that the Queen's stud was 'in a very bad state', chiefly because of the ignorance of the keepers who

45 *The riding house at Wolfeton House in Dorset, built probably by Sir George Trenchard, c. 1575–1600. The building, later converted into a barn, originally had windows in the right-hand wall as well as the gable end.*

'practise their profession merely by presuming that they know, and not by really knowing'. He found that neither stallions nor mares were given suitable fodder, because they were given grass that was too damp.

> When a foal, within its dam's body, is reared on damp grass which grows in such soil [as at Malmesbury], that wherever the mare puts her foot mire will rise and mix with the food, both the mare and the foal will become sluggish and heavy. A horse reared under such circumstances will have no strength.[29]

So far as breeding was concerned, Prospero's general principle was that 'to act contrary to nature is certainly against good judgment'. For this reason he disapproved of cross-breeds, particularly if they were the result of mating large animals with small. 'Bastards' is what he called them, insisting that none of them would have 'the back, speed, appearance, health and beauty that is found in ordinary breeds'. Stallions used for breeding should, he said, be at least thirteen years old, and kept for no other purpose, neither mounted, saddled nor harnessed. Young stallions, since their 'reproductive substance is like water', would produce only a sickly foal or nothing. As for brood mares, they should be at least five years old, and should on no account be covered every year, since 'even soil needs rest to produce good fruit'. The foals should be left with their dams for at least a year and a half, since that was both natural and good training for the foal. Finally, he insisted that the stallion should mount the mare without the help of man, preferably 'in a forest where they can run about together and get to know and like each other. This will make it possible for the mare to conceive perfectly and according to nature, since it is more her nature to be wild than domestic.' This last opinion was fully endorsed by Sir Thomas Blundeville in *The Foure Chiefest Offices belonging to Horsemanship*, first published in London in the mid 1560s. He explained with disapproval that if a mare refused the stallion, some people would try to force her

> by tieing her to a post set up in the midst of such a close yard or court as is talked of before, which thing is used even

at this present daie at Tutberie [Tutbury], whereat the Queenes Maiestie hath a race [i.e. stud]. And though I know that some of them do conceive and prosper well after it, yet I cannot praise it, because it is both dangerous and also unnatural.[30]

Not all of Prospero d'Osma's recommendations were followed. One of them, which was important, was that the Queen's establishment at Malmesbury (in West Park and Cole Park) should be closed down, so that the studs could be united at Tutbury where the grazing was not so uncomfortably wet. This was presumably resisted by the staff, for they were still at Malmesbury in 1596, even though they had allowed the establishment to run down badly.

> The parke is so ill fenced that the Coltes breake out and cover other mens mares. The rails and perticions are so ill that the horse coltes breake in amongst the mares and cover them. The parke gates are commonly left open as a common highwaye without locke . . . Also about the same parke there is not one paile standing, but hedged and ditched, which latly was ympayled rounde aboute. Also I lefte at my comminge from thence, beinge towardes the ende of June, fowre mares with fole, which sheweth that they were not gotten with fole by the stallions, but by the Coltes, as his [the keeper's] owne men doe partlie affirme.[31]

The keeper tried to excuse himself on grounds of ill health, but he was replaced, and his successor put the fences in order. Having done that – and this is an excellent example of the costliness of a good stud – he surrounded one of the two parks, Cole Park, with a dry stone wall 2,552 yards (2,331 m) long and 7 feet (2 m) high exclusive of the coping, all 'of sufficient height and strength for the keeping of horses and mares in the same park'. It was built in 1609–11 and cost £382.16s.8d.[32]

The most fascinating example of the extent to which the new attitude to horses had penetrated into England is to be found in a little book entitled *The Schoole of Horsemanship* by Christopher Clifford (London, 1585).[33] Though Clifford described himself as a 'gentleman', he spent most of his life as a mercenary soldier (sometimes as an officer but more often in the ranks) and as a glorified servant in charge of the horses of various English gentlemen. His contemporaries clearly found it difficult to place him socially, and he states repeatedly that he was illiterate, explaining that he dictated the first draft of his book to 'little Anthonie Bowser', standing on the cold stones in Master Throckmorton's stables at Tortworth (Gloucestershire). Nonetheless he had absorbed the essential teaching of Xenophon and Grisone, that horses should be treated with kindness and patience. What was more, he had the true spirit of scientific enquiry. Contemptuous of 'the learned fooles which carrie their science in their sachels and their wisdome in their lippes', he declared with an emphasis worthy of the Emperor Frederick II that the good rider, soldier, keeper or farrier 'must not recount what he hath read, but what he hath seene and done with his handes'.[34] When unable to establish the real cause of an illness from which a horse had died, he had no hesitation in conducting a *post-mortem* examination.

One of the *post-mortems* which he did was to establish that the horse's neck vein 'goeth right to the middle of the horse's heart, and spreadeth not abroad towards the necke and wythers, as some vaine horseleaches [horse-doctors] have presumed to teach me'.

> I gave a countrie man six pence, being on a colde frostie daie, to shew me an horse that was dead, . . . which horse I cut up in this order. Firstt I beganne with the necke vaine at the horses head, and put a small straight wand into the same, when I had put my rod as farre into the vaine as I could with my knife, I opened the same to the point thereof, so long till I thrust my rod by the same conduct into the middell of the horses heart, and afterwards returned to the arturie which lieth iust under the foresaide veine, and commeth into the middle of the heart also, and carrieth the vitall bloud to nourish the spirites withall, as they saie, which I doe not denie, and that veine, they saie, carrieth the nutrimentall bloud, which if they woulde leaue rolling in

their Rhetorike, and chopping of Logike, it were more proper in this arte to tearme it the bloud which nourisheth the bodie, for that wee ignorant groomes and horseleaches understand no such horseleaches Latine, nor eloquent termes whereby they do not onelie seeke to deceiue us, but a number of wise and learned Gentlemen, for the which I do not envie them so much.[35]

Though one cannot pretend that Clifford was anticipating the discoveries made by William Harvey *c.* 1619–28, he was clearly as up-to-date as most physicians of his time, if not more so. The fact is remarkable not only because he was illiterate, but also because in the previous centuries England had apparently received no veterinary texts whatsoever. Somehow or other, by inspiration or by conversation with other 'horseleaches' or gentry he had acquired the spirit of scientific investigation. He deserves to be remembered in England as much as Jordanus Ruffus in Italy. One of his employers, Sir John Tracy (one of the very few with whom he did not quarrel), reckoned his fame even higher, in commendatory verses which he wrote for the book.

> If Xenophon deserude immortall fame,
> Or Grisons glorie from earth to skie did reach,
> If Caraciolus gainde a worthy princely name,
> Whose Bookes the Art of Horsemanship doe teach,
> Then Cliffords praise what pen or tongue can tell,
> Whose paines herein, their works doth far excell.[36]

The Renaissance had certainly made an impact on the horsemen of England when such verses could be written about an illiterate 'groom or horseleach'.

It was fortunate that the advances in veterinary medicine and horsemanship occurred at a time when it was possible to acquire the types of bloodstock which were required to transform the best of the equine species into courtly horses. Forward-looking men like William Cavendish required medium-sized warhorses (above, p. 29) which were strong but also elegant, light and swift, in other words Arabians or Barbs or Spanish Jennets which carried much of   46 the blood of both. Since horsemen were now scientific they began to keep stud books. In England it is usually impossible at this date to tell the breed of those stallions and mares which had been bred in England, because they are identified simply by their former owners' names, but the foreign horses brought from abroad pose no such problems. At Hampton Court in 1620 there were six stallions, of which three were Barbs and one a Spanish Jennet.[37] In 1623 there were still six stallions, but now three of them were Jennets and two Barbs, and of the twenty-one mares they covered four were Spanish and two Barbs.[38] At Malmesbury in 1620 the five stallions consisted of a Turk, an ambling courser, a Jennet, a Barb and a Poland, and of the thirty-nine mares they covered four were Turks, two Arabians, three Jennets (and one other described as 'Spanish'), three Savoys, three Denmarks, two Polands and one a Friesland.[39] At Tutbury in 1624 the six stallions included one Arabian, one Barb, one Spanish and one 'French'. Of the forty-seven mares they covered eight were Polands, six Savoys, two Barbs, two 'Emperors' and one a Jennet.[40]

There is no means of telling what type of horse was the 'French' stallion at Tutbury, but the 'Polands' would have had Arabian or

46 Paragon, the favourite Barb of William Cavendish, from Cavendish's influential book, Méthode et Invention Nouvelle de dresser les Chevaux (Antwerp, 1658). The horse is evidently a portrait, but he could not have been at Welbeck before 1660: the exiled Cavendish probably acquired him at Paris in 1645–8.

Eastern blood because there were studs in Poland which, from the mid sixteenth century, specialized in breeding from horses captured or bought from the Turks. The Savoys would have come from the stud of the Duke of Savoy which is thought to have been based upon Spanish bloodstock at this date, because the Duke was married to the daughter of Philip II of Spain. The 'Emperors' were presumably from the stud of the Emperor Ferdinand II (1619–37) and therefore Lipizzaners, the stud at Lipizza (now Lipica) having been founded in 1576 with Spanish bloodstock. The 'Denmarks' would have been from the Danish royal stud at Frederiksborg which was founded in 1562 on (Spanish) Andalusians. Only the Friesland horse must be suspected of being on the heavy side and larger than the others.

At this point the transformation of the medieval warhorse into the English Thoroughbred must have seemed almost complete, as indeed it was, *almost*. The qualification is important because the English Civil War, which broke out in 1642, nearly destroyed the new breed. The best horsebreeders were Cavaliers – pre-eminent amongst them Charles I himself and his favourite George Villiers, Duke of Buckingham (d. 1628) who, as Master of the Horse, had

47

47 (below left) The image of kingly horsemanship: Charles I, by Van Dyck.
48 (below right) Sir Thomas Fairfax, portrayed not on his 'old grey mare' but on a large and fierce-looking stallion which, whether real or imaginary, is in the genuine tradition of the medieval warhorse.

been largely responsible for building up the royal studs. The Puritans, on the other hand, had a tendency to think that elegant foreign horses were amongst the trappings of royalty that had to be destroyed. They sold up studs whenever they could – that of William Cavendish in 1644 and the King's in 1649. Oliver Cromwell, as befitted a cavalryman, wanted to save the King's but was unable to do so. The horses were put up for sale in individual lots and the stud dispersed.

As a result of these disasters it used to be thought that the beginnings of the English Thoroughbred were to be found only after the Restoration as the work of Charles II and his courtiers. It is true that they did revive it, but they did not have to start from the very beginning. C. M. Prior was able to show that several of the mares from the royal stud at Tutbury were bought by James Darcy and taken to his stud at Sedbury near Gilling in North Yorkshire. 48 Others were rescued by Lord Fairfax, the Parliamentary commander, who lived in the same neighbourhood, and was himself a keen horsebreeder (he wrote a treatise on the subject). Not far from Fairfax's home at Nun Appleton was Helmsley, where the Duke of Buckingham had his stud. When Buckingham's lands were sequestered, Fairfax asked for and received Helmsley and its stud in lieu of arrears of pay; then, in order to secure it in the family, come what may, he married his daughter, who was his sole heir, to the second Duke of Buckingham. This was in 1657, while Oliver Cromwell was still alive and the Duke still officially in exile, but Fairfax weathered the storm and saw to it that some part of the 'royal race' of horses survived the Commonwealth and Civil War and could be continued into the Age of the Thoroughbred.[41] In an area far removed from the seat of central power, differences of politics or even allegiance had not prevented a small band of keen horsebreeders from co-operating in order to preserve a valuable breed of horses. The same sort of rescue operation must have been effected at frequent intervals during the Middle Ages. Otherwise the repeated dispersion of studs would have prevented the progress which, despite all interruptions, had made it possible first to make, and then to unmake, THE MEDIEVAL WARHORSE.

49,50 *Posthumous improvement. The final fall of the great horse from fashion is recorded in this pair of images. The first shows the original appearance of an early seventeenth-century picture of Henry, Prince of Wales; the second, the same canvas after overpainting is the late seventeenth century.*

The Prince was a noted supported of Renaissance equestrianism. Robert Peake portrayed him c. 1610 on a massive all-white horse, with Roman nose and ample breast and hindquarters. By the end of the century, it seems, not only the allegorical trappings (the Prince has secured Opportunity by the forelock) but the shape of the horse itself were thought hopelessly outmoded, and another painter was employed to transform the picture into someting resembling Van Dyck's Charles I *(Ill. 47): the mane was made thinner and dark, the nose straightened, and the neck and hindquarters trimmed down to give the animal the slimmer features of the new Thoroughbred. The story was discovered when the picture was cleaned.*

Abbreviations

ASC	*Anglo-Saxon Chronicle*, cited by year, *s.a.* (*sub anno*), so that reference can be made either to *Two of the Saxon Chronicles Parallel*, ed. Charles Plummer and John Earle (2 vols, Oxford, 1899) or to *The Anglo-Saxon Chronicle*, rev. trans. by Dorothy Whitelock with D. C. Douglas and S. I. Tucker (London, 1961)
BL	British Library, London
BN	Bibliothèque Nationale, Paris
Bautier	Anne-Marie and Robert-Henri Bautier, 'Contribution à l'histoire du cheval au Moyen Age', *Bulletin Philologique et Historique du Comité des Travaux historiques et scientifiques*, Paris, BN, *Année 1976*, 204–49, and *Année 1978*, 9–75
CCR	*Calendar of Close Rolls*
CPR	*Calendar of Patent Rolls*
Cap. Reg. Franc.	*Capitularia Regum Francorum*, ed. A. Boretius and V. Krause (2 vols, *MGH*, 1883–97)
Cavendish	William Cavendish (Duke of Newcastle), *A New Method and Extraordinary Invention to dress horses and work them according to Nature* (London, 1667). This is a revised edition of his *Méthode et Invention Nouvelle de dresser les chevaux* (Antwerp, 1658)
Chivers	Keith Chivers, *The Shire Horse: a History of the Breed, the Society and the Men* (London, 1976)
Contamine	Philippe Contamine, *War in the Middle Ages*, trans. Michael Jones (Oxford, 1984)
DB	*Domesday Book*, ed. Abraham Farley (2 vols, London, 1783)
DNB	*Dictionary of National Biography*
EHD	*English Historical Documents*, gen. ed. David C. Douglas (12 vols in 13, London, 1953—)
EHR	*English Historical Review*
Goodall	Daphne Machin Goodall, *A History of Horsebreeding* (London, 1977)
Huillard-Bréholles	*Historia Diplomatica Friderici II*, ed. J. L. A. Huillard-Bréholles (6 vols in 12, Paris, 1852–68)
Jankovich	Miklós Jankovich, *They Rode into Europe*, trans. Anthony Dent (London, 1971)
Jordanus	*Jordani Ruffi Calabriensis Hippiatria*, ed. Hieronimo [Girolamo] Molin (Padua, 1818)

MGH	*Monumenta Germaniae Historica*
Monast.	William Dugdale, *Monasticon Anglicanum*, new ed. by John Caley, Henry Ellis and Bulkeley Bandinel (6 vols in 8, London, 1817–30)
Moulé	Léon Moulé, *Histoire de la médecine vétérinaire* (3 vols in 4, Paris, 1891–1911) esp. *Deuxième Période*, pt 2, *Histoire de la médecine vétérinaire au moyen age (476–1500) . . . en Europe* (Paris, 1900)
Orderic	*The Ecclesiastical History of Orderic Vitalis*, ed. Marjorie Chibnall (6 vols, Oxford, 1969–80)
Poulle-Drieux	Y. Poulle-Drieux, 'L'Hippiatrie dans l'Occident Latin, du XIIIe au XVe siècle', in Guy Beaujouan, Yvonne Poulle-Drieux and Jeanne-Marie Dureau-Lapeyssonie, *Médecine humaine et vétérinaire à la fin du Moyen Age* (Geneva and Paris, 1966), 11–168
PR	Pipe Roll; refs. are to the editions printed by the Pipe Roll Society
PRO	Public Record Office
Prior (1924)	C. M. Prior, *Early Records of the Thoroughbred Horse* (London, 1924)
Prior (1935)	C. M. Prior, *The Royal Studs of the Sixteenth and Seventeenth Centuries* (London, 1935)
RS	Rolls Series
Reese	M. M. Reese, *The Royal Office of Master of the Horse* (London, 1976)
Ridgeway	(Sir) William Ridgeway, *The Origin and Influence of the Thoroughbred Horse* (Cambridge, 1905)
Roland	*The Song of Roland*, trans. Howard S. Robertson (London, 1972)
Rôles Gascons	*Rôles Gascons: Rôles de Edouard II, 1ère partie (1307–17)*, ed. Y. Renouard and R. Fawtier (Paris and London, 1962)
Rot. Lit. Claus.	*Rotuli Litterarum Clausarum in turri Londinensi asservati, 1204–27*, ed. T. D. Hardy (2 vols, London, 1833–44)
Rot. Lit. Pat.	*Rotuli Litterarum Patentium in turri Londinensi asservati, 1201–16*, ed. T. D. Hardy (London, 1835)
Settimane	*Settimane di Studio del Centro Italiano di Studi sull'Alto Medioevo* (Spoleto, 1953—)
SRG	*Scriptores rerum Germanicarum in usum scholarum (MGH)*
SRM	*Scriptores rerum Merovingicarum (MGH)*
Statutes of the Realm	*Statutes of the Realm (1101–1713)*, ed. A. Luders *et al.* (11 vols, London, 1810–28)
Thirsk	Joan Thirsk, *Horses in Early Modern England: for service, for pleasure, for power* (Stenton Lecture, 1977) (Reading, 1978)
Thompson	F. M. L. Thompson (ed.), *Horses in European Economic History, a Preliminary Canter*, British Agricultural History Society (Reading, 1983)
TRHS	*Transactions of the Royal Historical Society*

Notes

1 Medieval Cavalry Warfare

1 See below, nn. 8 and 10.

2 Werner's views, as well as those of his predecessors, are summarized in Contamine, 25.

3 R. H. C. Davis, *A History of Medieval Europe* (London, 1957), 141, from *Cap. Reg. Franc.*, i, no.75.

4 *Ernoul le Noir: Poème sur Louis le Pieux, et épîtres au Roi Pépin*, ed. E. Faral (Paris, 1932), bk ii, ll. 1116ff. and 1126ff. The famous equestrian statuette traditionally identified as Charlemagne, from Metz Cathedral (now in the Louvre), cannot be put forward in evidence either way: horse and rider were cast separately and seem to be of different dates (the rider is variously dated *c.* 810 and *c.* 860, and the horse is believed by some to be of *c.* 810 and by others as late as the sixteenth century). In any case the horse is not a destrier but a palfrey, the King/Emperor being shown in his robes of state rather than his armour.

5 Bernard S. Bachrach, 'Animals and Warfare in Early Medieval Europe', *Settimane*, xxxi (1983), 707–64; 'Charlemagne's Cavalry: Myth and Reality', *Military Affairs*, xlvii (1983), 181–7, with full bibliography.

6 *Annales Fuldenses*, ed. G. H. Pertz and F. Kurze (*SRG*, 1891), 120, 'quia Francis pedetemptim certare inusitatum est'.

7 Bachrach, 'Animals', 730. Bachrach translates the final sentence 'the charge was as bad as the battle', but the word 'charge' is an anachronism. What the annalist said was 'when they had got there badly, they also fought badly' – 'Quo cum esset male perventum, male etiam pugnatum est' (*Annales Regni Francorum*, ed. G. H. Pertz and F. Kurze (*SRG*, 1895), 63).

8 *The History of the Franks by Gregory of Tours*, trans. O. M. Dalton (2 vols, Oxford, 1927), ii, 90 (bk iii, ch. 7).

9 Quoted from Bachrach, 'Animals', 733.

10 *History of the Franks*, op. cit., ii, 199 (bk v, ch. 18 (25)).

11 The poets' 'clashing of shields' denoted more than the sound of swords and lances upon shields. It was more particularly the sound of shield upon shield as footsoldiers leapt at their opponents, endeavouring to pin them down with their shields while keeping the right hand free for a sword or knife. I have seen this demonstrated by Mr Alan Baxter and other members of the Dark Age Society. He assures me that such an attack could not be executed with the kite-shaped shields illustrated in the Bayeux Tapestry. Cf. Anna Comnena's account, quoted on p. 60.

12 Orderic, v, 257.

13 *Roland*, ll. 1379–85. For the meaning of the horses' names see p. 58.

14 The essential work for the lance and its use is François Buttin, 'La lance et l'arrêt de cuirasse', *Archaeologia*, 99 (1965), 77–178.

15 *Roland*, l. 1043: 'The lances shine, their wooden shafts upraised'.

16 *Chronica Rogeri de Houedene*, ed. William Stubbs (RS, 4 vols, 1868–71), iv, 58–9.

17 *Roland*, ll. 3152–4.

18 ibid., ll. 994–1001.

19 James F. Lydon, 'The Hobelar: an Irish Contribution to Medieval Warfare', *The Irish Sword*, ii, 5 (1954), 12–16; J. E. Morris, *Bannockburn* (Cambridge, 1914), 93–6.

20 Quoted from Malcolm Vale, *War and Chivalry* (London, 1981), 114.

21 Sir John Smythe, *Certain discourses . . . concerning the effects of divers sorts of weapons* (London, 1590), 4.

22 Cavendish, 77–8.

2 Origins and Methods of Horsebreeding

1 Sergei I. Rudenko, *Frozen Tombs of Siberia: the Pazyryk Burials of Iron Age Horsemen*, trans. M. W. Thompson (London, 1970), esp. 56–7.

2 *The Genius of China: an exhibition of the archaeological finds of the People's Republic of China, held at the Royal Academy, London, . . . from 29 September 1973 to 23 January 1974*, 110 and 118–21.

3 The great champion of the Libyan horse was William Ridgeway, who in *The Origin and*

Influence of the Thoroughbred Horse (Cambridge, 1905) insisted that it was due to the Greeks of North Africa who had crossed their small Homeric horses with zebras. See also Louis Mercier in his edition and translation of ʿAly Ben ʿAbderrahmen ben Hodeïl el Andalusy, *La Parure des cavaliers et l'insigne des preux* (Paris, 1924). For a different view John K. Anderson, *Ancient Greek Horsemanship* (Berkeley and Los Angeles, 1961), chs. 1 and 2, esp. p. 34.

4 A. H. M. Jones, *The Later Roman Empire, 284–602: a social and administrative survey* (3 vols and maps, Oxford, 1964), 706 and 768–9; Ridgeway, 257, nn. 1 and 2; Sidney D. Markham, *The Horse in Greek Art* (Baltimore, 1943), 6–10.

5 Jankovich, 37–8. See Appendix II.

6 Goodall, 123–5; Anderson, op. cit., 19.

7 Cavendish, 92.

8 Jankovich, 92. The surviving herds of feral horses in the USA are not so large, containing only ten to fifteen mares. See Appendix II.

9 ibid., 155, n.1.

10 Jordanus, 4.

11 Quoted in Chivers, 51.

12 *PR, 31 Henry I*, ed. Joseph Hunter (London, 1833, repr. 1929), 12.

13 *CCR, 1354–60*, 596. Haverah is near Fewston in the Forest of Knaresborough (West Yorkshire) and had been used as a stud at any rate since 1331; it is now known as 'John of Gaunt's Castle', having come into his possession in 1372 (H. M. Colvin, *The History of the King's Works* (London, 1963), ii, 671–3). Burstwick is in Holderness (East Yorkshire), 3 miles (5 km) east of Hedon, and was a well-known stud-farm.

14 Cavendish, 90–91.

15 ibid., 92, where he gives the figure as 2 out of 12, whereas in the French-language edition (1658, p. 24) he had given 3 out of 20.

16 Huntington Library, San Marino, Calif., Battle Abbey MSS: for Marley Farm, BA.477–9, 485, and 488–9; for Barnham BA.337, 346, 348 and 350. Cf. Eleanor Searle, *Lordship and Community: Battle Abbey and its Banlieu, 1066–1538* (Toronto, 1974), 293.

17 'Capitularia Missorum' of 819, *Cap. Reg. Franc.*, i, 219. In the twelfth century Orderic (v, 243) assumed that a horse which did not get its regular sester of oats 'could barely maintain its strength in western climes'.

18 The figures are taken from the *Equitium* accounts of Giles of Toulouse (PRO, E/101/99/19) and from D. Knoop and G. P. Jones, *The Medieval Mason* (Manchester, 1933), 236.

19 Chivers, 70–71, 293–311, 460–84.

20 ibid., 70.

21 T. C. Barker, 'The Delayed Decline of the Horse in the Twentieth Century', in Thompson, 101–12.

22 Chivers, 335–6.

23 Barker, op. cit., 109.

24 Chivers, 773.

25 ibid., 484.

26 ibid., 482.

27 ibid., 773.

3 The Revival of Horsebreeding in Western Europe

1 The letter, from Gregory's Register (ii, 32) is summarized in T. Hodgkin, *Italy and her Invaders* (8 vols in 9, Oxford, 1880–99), v, 317, from which these quotations are taken.

2 ibid., vi, 406.

3 Arbeo Frisingensis, 'Vita Corbiniani episcopi Baiuvariorum', ed. B. Krusch, *SRM*, vi (1913), 573 and 578–9.

4 Quoted by F. Viré in his article on 'Faras' in *Encyclopaedia of Islam* (new ed., London and Leiden, 1960—), ii, 786.

5 Pliny, *Hist. Nat.*, viii, 166. Cf. Ridgeway, 257, nn. 1 and 2. There seems to be an echo of this legend in *The Cid*, which relates how the Cid chose his horse, Babieca, because unlike other horses he stood facing the wind instead of turning his tail to it.

6 See, for example, D. A. Bullough in *EHR*, 85 (1970), 84–9, and Bernard S. Bachrach, 'Animals and Warfare in Early Medieval Europe', *Settimane*, xxxi (1983), 707–64.

7 H. R. Loyn and John Percival, *The Reign of Charlemagne* (London, 1975), 148: 'equum obtimum et brunia obtima et spatia India cum techa de argento parata'.

8 Bautier (1978), 16–20.

9 *Einhard and Notker the Stammerer: two lives of Charlemagne*, trans. Lewis Thorpe (Harmondsworth, 1969), 147 (bk ii, ch. 9).

10 *Cap. Reg. Franc.*, i, 84, and following in the main the translation in Loyn and Percival, op. cit., 66–7. The 'winter palace' was wherever the

king/emperor happened to be spending the winter.

11 *Cap. Reg. Franc.*, i, 190, para. 7; Loyn and Percival, op. cit., 50.

12 Paul the Deacon, *Hist. Langobardorum* (ed. G. Waitz, *SRG* (1878), p. 91); *Ernoul le Noir: Poème sur Louis le Pieux, et épîtres au Roi Pépin*, ed. E. Faral (Paris, 1932), bk ii, ll. 1116–17 and 1126–7.

13 *Cap. Reg. Franc.*, ii, 321, para. 25. During the ninth century *caballus* was the standard word for warhorse. (See the Glossary.)

14 *Ernoul le Noir*, op. cit., pp. 22–4. Faral dates the incident to 793, when the Saracens are known to have been in Septimania (Southern France between the Rhône and Narbonne). I owe this reference to Mr James Campbell.

15 Inquisition on the tolls of Rafelstetten, 903–6, in *Cap. Reg. Franc.*, ii, 251.

16 Jankovich, 94.

17 K. Leyser, 'Henry I and the beginning of the Saxon Empire', *EHR*, 83 (1968), 1–32 (esp. 5–6, 15–22 and 25), reprinted in his *Medieval Germany and its Neighbours, 900–1250* (London, 1982), 11–42.

18 *Guillaume de Jumièges – Gesta Ducum Normannorum*, ed. Jean Marx (Soc. de l'histoire de Normandie, Rouen and Paris, 1914), 106–8.

19 This paragraph and the next summarize my findings published in 'The Warhorses of the Normans', *Anglo-Norman Studies*, x (1987), in which full references are given.

20 *Roland*, ll. 1490–96; for Tencendur, ll. 2993–5. For horses in the *chansons de geste* generally, see Léon Gautier, *La Chevalerie* (Paris, 1896), 722–9 n.

21 *Gaufredus Malaterra: De Rebus Gestis Rogerii Calabriae et Siciliae Comitis et Roberti Guiscardi ducis fratris eius*, ed. E. Pontieri (*Rerum Italicarum Scriptores*, Bologna, 1928), bk i, ch. 9 (p. 12). Cf. John Julius Norwich, *The Normans in the South* (London, 1967), 60–61.

22 *Guillaume de Pouille: la Geste de Robert Guiscard*, ed. Marguerite Mathieu (Palermo, 1961), 140 (bk ii, ll. 153–7).

23 *The Alexiad of Anna Comnena*, trans. E. R. A. Sewter (Harmondsworth, 1969), 171, 349, 416. Anna was writing in the 1140s.

24 Contamine, 55.

25 *L'Histoire de Guillaume le Maréchal*, ed. Paul Meyer (Soc. de l'histoire de France, Paris, 3 vols, 1891–1901), ll. 2933–5.

26 Huillard-Bréholles, v, 525.

27 ibid., v, 865–6.

28 John H. Pryor, 'Transportation of horses by sea during the era of the crusades: eighth century to 1288 A.D.', *The Mariner's Mirror*, 68 (1982), 'pt i, to *c.* 1223', pp. 9–30, and 'pt ii, 1228–1285', pp. 103–25. I owe this reference to Mr Bill Ringler.

29 Boccaccio, *Decameron*, Day 2, Novel 5.

30 Alan Ryder, *The Kingdom of Naples under Alfonso the Magnanimous* (Oxford, 1976), 70–71.

31 Gualvanei de la Flamma in *Rerum Italicarum Scriptores*, xii, pt iv (Bologna, 1938), 41–2; *CCR 1231–4*, 96; *CPR 1272–81*, 191; Thomas Rymer, *Foedera* (20 vols, London, 1704–35), iii, 124.

32 Bautier (1978), 63–8.

33 ibid., 68–9 and 60–61.

34 *Materials for the History of Thomas Becket*, ed. James Craigie Robertson (RS, 7 vols, London, 1875–85), iii, 6).

35 For agricultural horses see John Langdon, *Horses, Oxen and Technological Invention: the use of draught animals in English farming from 1066–1500* (Cambridge, 1986).

4 Horsebreeding in Medieval England

1 *Bedae Historia Ecclesiastica Gentis Anglorum*, ed. Charles Plummer (Oxford, 1896), i, 156 (bk 3, ch. 14).

2 *Beowulf*, ed. and trans. Michael Swanton (Manchester, 1978), ll. 1036–43.

3 F. L. Attenborough, *The Laws of the Earliest English Kings* (Cambridge, 1922, repr. New York, 1963), 44–5; or *EHD*, i, p. 367, ch. 29.

4 *EHD*, i, no. 95, p. 491.

5 Cf. J. H. Clapham, 'The Horsing of the Danes', *EHR*, 25 (1910), 287–93.

6 *ASC*, s.a. 897 (= 896).

7 Attenborough, op. cit., 136–7 (II Athelstan, 16 and 18); *EHD*, i, p. 384.

8 F. E. Harmer, *Select English Historical Documents of the ninth and tenth centuries* (Cambridge, 1914), 33, 63 and 116ff.

9 Dorothy Whitelock, *Anglo-Saxon Wills* (Cambridge, 1930), 6–7.

10 ibid., 58–61.

11 Arthur S. Napier and William H. Stevenson, *The Crawford Collection of Early Charters*

and Documents now in the Bodleian Library (Oxford, 1895), no. x.

12 Whitelock, op. cit., 32–3.

13 ibid., 82–3.

14 *EHD*, i, no. 50, p. 429 (Clauses 71, 71a, 71.1).

15 *EHD*, i, no. 10, esp. p. 296. The date of the poem is usually thought to be close to 991, the year of the battle (Eric John, 'War and Society in the Tenth Century: the Maldon Campaign', *TRHS*, 5th ser., xxvii (1977), 173–95, esp. n. 61), but it *could* be considerably later.

16 Richard Glover, 'English Warfare in 1066', *EHR*, 67 (1952), 1–18.

17 Sir Frank Stenton, *Anglo-Saxon England* (3rd ed., Oxford, 1971), 640.

18 L. M. Larson, *The King's Household in England before the Norman Conquest* (Madison, Wis., 1904), 147.

19 F. E. Harmer, *Anglo-Saxon Writs* (Manchester, 1952), 51. The Scandinavian origin is still defended by Pamela Nightingale in *EHR*, 102 (1987), 564–6, though she apparently accepts Harmer's chronology. She attempts to link the office with London exclusively, though to my mind such a theory makes it difficult to explain why several stallers were serving at once.

20 L. M. Larson, *Canute the Great* (New York and London, 1912), 282.

21 *ASC, s.a.* 1067 (D). See also E. A. Freeman, *The History of the Norman Conquest* (6 vols, Oxford, 1876–9), iv, Appendix N.

22 *The Life of King Edward the Confessor*, ed. Frank Barlow (London, 1970), 76.

23 *DB*, i, ff. 218b and 151.

24 ibid., 347b–348.

25 John Clark, *Medieval Horseshoes*, Finds Research Group 700–1700, Datasheet 4 (Coventry Museums, n.d. [*c*. 1986]).

26 Bernard S. Bachrach, 'Some Observations on the Military Administration of the Norman Conquest', *Anglo-Norman Studies*, viii (1985), 1–25, esp. 12. There are several difficulties about his figures; e.g. how can a requirement of 14–20 tons a day add up to a total of 1,500 tons a month? And how can a horse which eats 25 lb (11 kg) of grain and hay produce 65–70 lb (29–32 kg) of faeces?

27 *DB*, i, f. 57b. But Walter Fitz Other, Castellan of Windsor, also held land there, free of all customs 'because of his custody of the forest' (i.e. of Windsor): *DB*, i, f. 61b.

28 The figures are taken from H. C. Darby, *Domesday England* (Cambridge, 1977, repr. 1986), 164.

29 *DB*, i, f. 36.

30 ibid., ii, ff. 173, 179b, 178 and 180.

31 For a map and list of the 35 parks, see Darby, op. cit., 202–3. The 13 parks specifically for wild beasts were Stagsden (Bedfordshire), Long Crendon (Buckinghamshire), Burrough Green and Kirtling (Cambridgeshire), Winkleigh (Devon), Bishop's Waltham (Hampshire), Bennington, St Albans and Ware (Hertfordshire), Chart Sutton (Kent), Ruislip (Middlesex), Costessy (Norfolk) and Hollow Green (Worcestershire).

32 Charles G. O. Bridgeman, 'The Burton Abbey Surveys', *Collections for a History of Staffordshire* (William Salt Soc.), 41 (1916), 212, 228.

33 *Monast.*, i, 629.

34 *The Cartulary of Shrewsbury Abbey*, ed. Una Rees (2 vols, Aberystwyth, 1975), pp. 34, 39, 42.

35 Above, Ch. 2, n. 12.

36 *Charters of the Honour of Mowbray, 1107–1191*, ed. D. E. Greenway (London, 1972), no. 52 (p. 40).

37 *PR, 11 Henry II*, 109, and *12 Henry II*, 115.

38 *PR, 12 Henry II*, 59; R. W. Eyton, *Antiquities of Shropshire* (12 vols, London, 1853–60), ii, 108–20.

39 *PR, 22 Henry II*, 58.

40 *PR, 17 Henry II*, 29; *25 Henry II*, 14, 92; *26 Henry II*, 96.

41 *PR, 23 Henry II*, 81; *27 Henry II*, 47.

42 For the papal legate's palfrey, *PR, 23 Henry II*, 47. For the expensive horse, *PR, 25 Henry II*, 83.

43 *PR, 18 Henry II*, 7, 13, 18, 21, 40, 72, 89, 103, 107, 119, 124, 129.

44 ibid., 72, and *PR, 19 Henry II*, 108, where 53s. 4d. is paid for shipping the King's horses. As the cost worked out at 6d. a horse in the previous year, this sum suggests a further 106 horses.

45 *Itinerarium . . . Regis Ricardi*, in *Chronicles and Memorials of the Reign of Richard I*, ed. W. Stubbs (2 vols, RS, 1864), i, 419, and for the shipping i, 192. Also *Ambroise: The Crusade of Richard the Lion-Hearted*, trans. Merton J. Hunt with notes by John L. Lamonte (New York, 1941), ll. 11549ff.

46 *Rot. Lit. Claus.*, i, 51, 67, 81, 94, 98.
47 *PR, 14 John*, 27, 58, 129, 130; cf. *Rot. Lit. Claus.*, i, 121.
48 *Rot. Lit. Claus.*, i, 150, 175, 180, 181, 188, 190, 213, and *PR, 16 John*, 27, and *17 John*, 41.
49 *Rot. Lit. Claus.*, i, 40.
50 *CPR 1225–32*, 139, 141; *CPR 1258–66*, 139, 143, 158, 284, 444.
51 *CCR 1237–42*, 502, 529, and *CPR 1232–47*, 342.
52 *CCR 1231–4*, 96, and *CPR 1232–47*, 242.
53 *CPR 1258–64*, 121.
54 *CPR 1272–81*, 169, 171 bis, 184 bis, 191, 193, 194. It is sometimes difficult to know whether various letters are referring to the same or different batches of horses. I have taken the 20 horses brought over by Matthew de Columbariis on 12 December 1276 to be different from those which he had on 6 February 1277; and the 20 which Nutus de Florentia had on 15 November 1276 not to include the 10 which he had on 12 December 1276.
55 *Parliamentary Writs*, ed. Francis Palgrave (2 vols in 4, London, 1827–34), i, 226, no. 9.
56 H. M. Colvin, *The History of the King's Works* (London, 1963), ii, 919.
57 *Letters of Edward Prince of Wales, 1304–5*, ed. Hilda Johnstone (Roxburghe Club, cxciv, 1931), 1, 2, 31.
58 *CPR 1307–13*, 124; and Thomas Rymer, *Foedera*, iii, 124.
59 *CPR 1307–13*, 204, 437; *Foedera*, iii, 394–5; *Rôles Gascons*, nos 1378, 1225; and PRO E/101/99/20.
60 PRO E/101/101/10.
61 Wendy Childs, *Anglo-Castilian Trade in the Later Middle Ages* (Manchester, 1978), 120–21; but Spanish horses were still being imported in 1342 (*CCR 1341–3*, 595).
62 *CCR 1341–3*, 44.
63 PRO E/101/105/8 and 29.
64 *CPR 1361–4*, 370.
65 PRO E/101/99/27.
66 PRO E/101/105/12.
67 PRO E/101/99/22 (Beauxamys); *CPR 1354–8*, 111, 285, 603 (Fremelsworth); *CPR 1354–8*, 116, 324, and *CCR 1354–60*, 559 (Rose); *CCR 1354–60*, 596 (Botha).
68 PRO E/101/102/35 (Oct. 1344); E/101/103/30 (dorse) (22 May 1348); E/101/104/5 (1350–51); E/101/105/8 (1357); E/101/105/12 (1358) and E/101/105/33 (1360) and Montagu

Burrows, *The Family of Brocas of Beaurepaire* (London, 1886), 59ff.
69 Burrows, op. cit., 82ff. and Burrows's article on Sir Bernard Brocas in *DNB*.
70 *CPR 1381–5*, 307. This is the earliest date (13 Sept. 1383) at which I have found the title, though Reese, 340, dates Moreaux's tenure 'circa 1377'.
71 Reese, 340–42, with minor corrections to some dates.
72 *Statutes of the Realm*, ii, 518.

5 The Impact of the Renaissance

1 For veterinary medicine the essential works, on which I have relied throughout, are Poulle-Drieux and Moulé.
2 Quoted from his *Quaestiones Naturales* in R. W. Southern, *Robert Grosseteste: the Growth of an English Mind in the Middle Ages* (Oxford, 1986), 86.
3 Quoted from Thomas Curtis Van Cleeve, *The Emperor Frederick II of Hohenstaufen* (Oxford, 1972), 314.
4 Moulé, ii, pt 2, 25.
5 *Jordani Ruffi Calabriensis Hippiatria*, ed. Hieronymus [Girolamo] Molin (Padua, 1818). Poulle-Drieux has established that the Latin version is the original, and the Italian, Sicilian, French, Provençal and Catalan versions translations of it. She also gives lists of manuscripts and printed editions which improve greatly on the pioneering (and still valuable) work of Moulé, ii, pt 2, 25–30.
6 Huillard-Bréholles, i, dxxxvii.
7 Jordanus, 1.
8 Jordanus, 2–4.
9 Poulle-Drieux, 15–21. In fact she lists 20 Latin manuscripts, but Merton MS. 230 is an old reference for Merton MS. 1234. I have omitted the latter also, because the text concerned is not that of Jordanus, even though it bears some relationship to it.
10 *The Surgery of Theodoric, ca. A.D. 1267*, trans. Eldridge Campbell and James Colton (2 vols, New York, 1955–6); *Die Pferdeheilkunde Bischoffs Theodorich von Cervia*, Abhandlung i by E. Dolz (Berlin, 1937; veter. inaug. dissert. 1734); Abh. ii by G. Klutz (Berlin, 1936; veter. inaug. dissert. 1722); Abh. iii by

W. Heinemeyer (Berlin, 1936; veter. inaug. dissert. 1743). Poulle-Drieux, 22–4.

11 Poulle-Drieux, 29–30.

12 ibid., 35.

13 ibid., 40–43. The (medieval) Italian and Latin texts are printed on facing pages in *La Mascalcia di Lorenzo Rusio*, ed. Pietro Delprato and Luigi Barbieri (2 vols, Bologna, 1867). For Laurentius's patron, see Carl Arnold Willemsen, *Kardinal Napoleon Orsini (1263–1343)* (*Historische Studien*, Heft 172, Berlin, 1927). Apparently there is a further manuscript of Laurentius's work in New York: Pierpont Morgan Library, MS. 735.

14 Poulle-Drieux, 36–8; Manuel Díaz, *Libro de Albeyteria, es a saber de los caballos y da las mulas* (Saragossa, 1495).

15 Poulle-Drieux, 115.

16 ibid., 46–7, with partial edition of the text on 123–48.

17 Jordanus, 1.

18 Jocelyne G. Russell, *The Field of Cloth of Gold: men and manners in 1520* (London, 1969), 118–19.

19 Thirsk, 8–9.

20 *Statutes of the Realm*, iii, 535 and 758. Cf. Sir Walter Gilbey, *The Great Horse or Shire Horse* (2nd ed., London, 1899), 24. The shires named in the Act of 1540 were: Norfolk, Suffolk, Cambridge, Buckingham, Huntingdon, Essex, Kent, Southam[pton]shire, 'Northwilshire', Oxford, Berkshire, Worcester, Gloucester, Somerset, Bedford, Warwick, Northampton, Yorkshire, Cheshire, Staffordshire, Lancaster, Shropshire, Leicester, Hereford and Lincoln; the districts were North Wales, South Wales, the County and City of York, the Town and Liberties of Gloucester, and the County of the Town of Kingston-upon-Hull.

21 *Statutes of the Realm*, iii, 830–31.

22 Thirsk, 14–17, for the whole of this subject. See also A. F. Pollard's article on Sir Nicholas Arnold in the DNB, First Suppl. (xxii, 75–6).

23 *Xenophon in Seven Volumes*, ed. and trans. E. C. Marchant (Loeb Classical Library, Cambridge, Mass. and London, 1934), vii, 296–363. For manuscripts and editions see also Edouard Delbecq, *Xenophon: de l'art équestre* (Paris, 1978) and R. R. Bolgar, *The Classical Heritage and its Beneficiaries* (Cambridge, 1958, repr. 1977), 492–4.

24 Grisone as rendered by Blundeville, quoted from the edition of 1580, bk ii (*The Art of Riding*), f. 5v. Blundeville first published his translation and adaptation of Grisone as *A newe booke containing the arte of ryding and breakinge great Horses*, probably *c.* 1560. Its favourable reception by 'the moste part of the Ientlemen of this Realme' encouraged him, he tells us, to add to it three other books, on the offices of the Breeder (bk i), the Keeper (bk iii, on diet, dated 1565), and the Ferrer (bk iv, on diseases and farriery, dated 1566). This enlarged work was called *The fower chiefyst offices belonging to Horsemanshippe*. It in turn was so successful that it was republished after 1571, in 1580, and later. Each of the four books has its separate foliation.

25 Translated (with editorial modification) by Sir John Astley, *The Art of Riding* (London, 1584), 17.

26 Blundeville (1580), bk ii, f. 28. For the editions of Blundeville see above, n. 24.

27 Sir Thomas Bedingfield, *The Art of Riding according to Claudio Corte* (London, 1584), 8.

28 *Inventory of the Historical Monuments in the County of Dorset*, iii, *Central Dorset* (Royal Commission on Historical Monuments, London, 1970), pp. lix and 68–9.

29 Prospero's report is printed and translated in Prior (1935), 11–38; this quotation, 23–4, the rest from 30, 33 and 35–7.

30 Blundeville (1580), bk i, f. 14v. (See above, n. 24.)

31 Prior (1935), 64.

32 ibid., 66.

33 The book is very rare. The British Library's copy is defective and the only two complete copies are in the United States, at (i) the Huntington Library, San Marino, Calif. (which I have used), and (ii) the Folger Library in Washington. Christopher Clifford was a fascinating and mysterious person, about whom I intend to write more elsewhere.

34 Clifford, f. 63v.

35 ibid., ff. 63v–64.

36 ibid., f. iii.

37 Prior (1935), 39–40.

38 ibid., 40–41.

39 ibid., 66–8.

40 ibid., 48–9.

41 Prior (1924), 5–7, and Prior (1935), *passim*.

Appendix I

Jordanus on How to Judge the Beauty of a Horse

In the fourth chapter of his book (see above, pp. 101–3) Jordanus explains how to judge the beauty of a horse. As it is the only such description by a medieval 'vet' it is extremely interesting, but it also illustrates the difficulty of translating 'horse-Latin'. It should be remembered that Jordanus's own language would have been Italian or Sicilian, but there are apparently two different words indicating the hock, and four indicating the thigh, loin, hip or buttock.

In the first place the horse's body should have substance and length, with all the other limbs in proportion. The horse's head should be long, slender and fine, the mouth big and lacerated [*laceratum*],[1] the nostrils large and inflated, the eyes wide and protruding, the ears small and like shields [*aspideas*]. He should display [*obtulat*][2] a long neck, strongly set on [*bene*] towards the head, with cheeks well defined and firm, having few [long] hairs. The breast should be well developed and rounded and should present [*obtulat*][2] a prominent feature [*guarensem*][3] which is not narrow but tense and flat. The back [*dorsum*] should be short and more-or-less level, the loins [*lumbos*][4] well-fleshed and broad, the ribs wide-sprung and the upper thighs [*ilia*] like those of an ox. [The horse] should have a long belly [*ventrem*], haunches [*ancas*][5] long and tense, the croup [*clunem*][6] equally long and full. The tail [*cauda*][7] should be broad [*grossa*] with few and flat hairs [*cum paucis et planis crinibus*]. I say it should have upper thighs [*coxas*][8] which are broad and full, and lower thighs [*garecta*][9] fairly full, tense and firm. The hocks [*falces*][10] should be curved and full like those of a deer. The legs should be very ample, hairy and firm, the fetlock joints [*juncturas crurium*] broad but not too fleshy, nor too close to the hooves in the manner of oxen. The feet or hooves should be ample, hard and concave, as I have said. The horse should also be a little taller at the back than at the front, like a deer. It should hold its neck high, viz. with the thickness nearest to the body. And anyone who wishes to understand the beauty of a horse correctly must see that the aforesaid limbs are formed in proportion to both the height and the length of the horse.

[1] It is not clear why the mouth should be 'lacerated'. Perhaps he means that it should be sufficiently tender to have been lacerated by the bit.
[2] *obtulat* seems, on the face of it, to be a confusion between *offerat* and its aorist, *obtulit*.
[3] *guarensem*. I have been driven to the conclusion that this must be connected with *waranio*, the ninth-century word for a stallion (see p. 52 above, and Glossary), and also with the (now obsolete) English word 'yard' which indicated the virile member.
[4] *lumbus* is the normal Latin word for a loin, but the context suggests buttocks.
[5] *anca* is the Italian, Provençal, Spanish and Portuguese word for the hip or buttock. Our word 'haunch' is derived from it.
[6] *clune* is the Italian word for buttocks, but since Jordanus uses it in Latin in the singular I have suggested 'croup'.
[7] *cauda* is the normal Latin word for 'tail', but it is hard to see why it should have few hairs. He presumably means that it should be groomed so as not to be too fuzzy.
[8] *coxa* is the normal Latin word for hip-bone. The French *cuisse* which is derived from it signifies the thigh or loin.
[9] *garecta* is presumably the same as the Italian *garetto*, indicating the hock of a horse or ankle of a man, though here the context demands lower thigh (gaskin).
[10] *falx* is the Latin word for a scythe or pruning-hook, but in Italian *falce* indicates the hock of a horse.

Appendix II

Feral Horses

Feral horses are wild horses whose ultimate ancestry is known to have been in domesticated breeds.[1] The best examples are to be found in North America, where (after about 7000 BC) no horses were known until the Spanish and later colonists brought them across the Atlantic. Some of these horses escaped and formed herds in the uncolonized wastes. Large numbers of them survived until the twentieth century when man began to pursue them into their remote homelands in the Rockies or the barrier islands off the East Coast of Pennsylvania, Maryland and North Carolina. Since 1970, and largely because of the publicity given to them by Hope Ryden, the remaining herds have been protected by law.[2] They have also become the object of much scientific observation which is very relevant to our main theme, because feral horses offer the best possible demonstration of the dangers of 'losing the breed'. They also enable us to comprehend the natural behaviour of the wild or woodland mares of the Middle Ages.

Feral horses are pony-sized and develop zebra-like stripes (often quite faint) on their legs. They move about in herds each of which normally consists of a stallion and his harem of ten to fifteen mares together with their foals. Observers in previous centuries talk of much larger herds; in 1838 Don Felix de Azara stated that the wild horses of Paraguay congregated together in such numbers 'that it is no exaggeration to say that they sometimes amount to twelve thousand individuals'.[3] We may not believe this number, but we have to concede that when there was very much more wild pasture available the herds could well have been larger than they are now.

Reverting to the present herds, it has been observed that the mares are fertile from the age of three to seventeen, the maximum fertility being at the age of seven. In the Granite Range in Nevada at a time (1979–83) when the grazing was exceptionally good, at least 83% of the mares aged five to seventeen gave birth to four foals over a five-year period, but of these foals 8% did not live a year, and 3% died in their second year. In other places the fertility rate of the mares has been calculated at a little under 60% (59.6% on Sable Island), the most important factor being the quantity and quality of the grazing.[4] On Assateague Island (like Sable Island, off the East Coast) the herds on the northern half are completely unmanaged and have a fertility rate of 57.1%. On the southern half they are managed to the extent that all foals and fillies are moved from their dams before the onset of their first winter, and the fertility rate of the mares is increased to 74.4% because, no longer having to nurse their young, they retain all the nourishment of their grazing. As for the offspring which have been removed, they are fed a daily ration of 1 lb (0.45 kg) of grain for every 100 lb (45 kg) of body-weight, with as much hay as they require. They lose no weight over the winter, and grow taller and heavier than their contemporaries on the northern part of the island.[5]

Broadly speaking, feral mares can be expected to give birth to nine or ten offspring in their lifetime. Gestation lasts eleven months and the foals are generally born in April, May or June (more than half of them in May itself) when there is plenty of grass in the fields. The foals will have been weaned after six months but (when not managed by man) will run with their dams for about two years. Though the numbers of male and female births are about equal, the stallion does not tolerate other male adults in his herd. Consequently the young males will break away or be driven out when they are two years old, and will roam singly or in pairs, hoping to acquire some females of their own by successfully challenging a stallion. The majority of

133

these 'bachelors' have no success and die early, either from injuries incurred in a stallion fight or (more commonly) from malnutrition since, lacking the protection of a herd, they are continually interrupted in their grazing.

Feral horses are awake for twenty to twenty-two hours of the day and spend 70% of their time (forty-two minutes in every hour) grazing. In winter when the grass is scanty their grazing time increases to 80% (or forty-eight minutes in every hour). If the herd is harassed by stray males, other animals or humans, feeding time will be lost; the leading mare will guide the herd out of harm's way, while the stallion comes up from the rear to do battle. The amount of grazing time lost by such disturbances can amount to as much as two hours a day, which would be 9 or 10% of the total feeding time.[6] The strongest stallions (who will also have the largest harem) usually succeed in reducing these disturbances by establishing a territory of their own and keeping all other horses off it. The herd will then move around its territory systematically. Herds with established territories can be found not only in the USA but also in England, on Exmoor and in the New Forest where wild or woodland mares roamed in the Middle Ages.

[1] I am very grateful to Professor Daniel I. Rubenstein who gave me much assistance while he was a Visiting Fellow at Merton College, Oxford.

[2] Hope Ryden, *Wild Horses* (London, 1972), an attractive introduction.

[3] The quotation, as well as the facts from the Granite Range, given below, comes from Joel Berger, *Wild Horses of the Great Basin* [in north-eastern Nevada]: *Social Competition and Population Size* ('Wild Life Behaviour and Ecology' series, ed. George B. Scheller, Chicago and London, 1986), esp. 10.

[4] ibid., 76. W. M. Dawson, R. W. Phillips and S. R. Speelman, in 'Growth of Horses under Western Range Conditions' [in Montana], *Journal of Animal Science*, 4 (1945), 47–54, show that in the decisive first two years of their life, foals depending entirely on the grazing available on the range would gain up to 250 lb (113 kg) in summer but lose up to 100 lb (45 kg) in winter. Those provided with winter fodder would lose no weight at all, but rather gain a little.

[5] Ronald Keiper and Katherine Houpt, 'Reproduction in Feral Horses: An Eight-year Study', *American Journal of Veterinary Research*, 45 (1984), 991–5.

[6] Daniel I. Rubenstein, 'Ecology and Sociality in Horses and Zebras', in Daniel I. Rubenstein and Richard W. Wrangham, *Ecological Aspects of Social Evolution: Birds and Mammals* (Princeton, N.J., 1986), 282–302.

The best and fullest glossary is by Anne-Marie Bautier, 'Le Vocabulaire du cheval en Latin médiéval', in Bautier 1976. My aim here has been to list those words, whether Latin or not, which proved troublesome to me in the writing of this book.

Colours are listed separately at the end.

Affer, afrus, averius, averus, avrus: the cheapest form of farm horse.

Albeitaria, albeyteria (Catalan); a vet; probably derived from Ibn el-Baithar, the Arab pharmacist (d. 1248).

Alfaracis, alferaz (Sp., from the Arabic *al faras*, the horse): used for good horses such as destriers in Spain from the ninth century. In Romance *aufferant*. See also *haracium*.

Ambulatorius (*equus*): an ambler or pacing horse, which moves by lifting the two feet on one side together, alternately with the two feet on the other. See also *gradarius*, the French *haquenai*, and the twelfth-century description quoted above, p. 45.

Anusus: a colt in its first year, usually unweaned and following its dam.

Barb, Barbary horse: a breed of horse from the 'Barbary', or Berber, coast of the Mediterranean (Libya, Tunisia, Algeria and Morocco), and rather smaller than the Arabian. The term *equus de Barbaria* occurs in letters of the Emperor Frederick II in 1240. In England the term 'Barb' is first found in 1636.

Caballus: in Classical Latin this word denoted an inferior riding horse or even a packhorse, but from the sixth to the tenth or eleventh centuries it denoted a good horse, usually a warhorse. In Southern France and Spain it retained this meaning, but in North-Western Europe, Italy and Germany it was superseded by other words such as *equus* or destrier. It is rarely found in England at all. From it are derived the normal words for 'horse', 'knight' and 'chivalry' in French, Italian and Spanish (e.g. *cheval, chevalier, chevalerie* and *cavallo, cavaliere, cavalleria*). The English words 'cavalier' and 'chivalry' are derived not directly from the Latin but from the Italian and French respectively, occurring first in 1560 and *c*. 1590.

Carectarius, carettarius: a carthorse.

Catzurius, cazorius, chazurius: a hunter, or horse for the chase; used in England from the end of the twelfth century. Cf. *cursarius*.

Cob: a short-legged, stout type of horse for riding. Not a special breed, nor a technical term before the nineteenth century.

Cornipes: a horse (a very literary word, used by chroniclers such as Orderic Vitalis). Cf. *sonipes*.

Cursarius: a courser or swift riding horse; occurs in England mainly from the fourteenth century onwards. Possibly a variant of *catzurius* (q.v.).

Dextrarius (Fr. *destrier*): a warhorse. Perhaps so called because, when not in battle, it was led by a squire on his right hand.

Emissarius (*equus*): a stallion (a horse which emits); a term used mainly from the fourth to the ninth centuries on the Continent, but found occasionally in England from the twelfth to fourteenth centuries. Cf. *waranio*

Equaricia: a stud

Faras (Arabic), *farius equus*: a horse, quite possibly an Arabian. See *alfaracis*.

Fugator: a courser or swift riding horse suitable for hunting. A term used from the twelfth century, but driven out of use in the fourteenth century by *cursarius* (q.v.).

Gelding: a castrated horse. So far as warhorses and good riding horses were concerned, it is broadly true to say that though geldings were used by the Arabs and Turks and in Eastern Europe generally, they were little used in the West until the sixteenth century. That is why the French call a gelding a 'Hungarian' (*hongre*) horse, and the Germans call it a Wallachian (*Wallach*). Marx Fugger (*Von der Gestüterey*, Frankfurt-am-Main, 1584, p. 37) quoted Albertus Magnus to the effect that castration made horses timid and therefore unsuited for war, but added that the Turks, Muscovites and Tartars did use geldings and continued to defeat the Christians. Jordanus Ruffus (*c.* 1256) knew about castration but recommended it only when medically necessary. In medieval England geldings seem to have been used in a lowly way. At the end of the fourteenth century Chaucer disdainfully likened the pardoner to a 'geldyng or a mare'. In the sixteenth century there was a change; Thomas Blundeville stated that in England light horsemen used geldings in the wars, but added that they were used 'partly for their servants to ride on and to carie their male [i.e. trunk] and cloke bagges after them' (Blundeville (1580), bk i, f. 19).

Gradarius: a pacing horse. See *ambulatorius*.

Haquenai (Fr.), *hakene* (ME). Though the modern Hackney has both Arab and Thoroughbred blood in its veins, the *haquenai* is recorded at least as early as 1300, more than three centuries earlier than the Thoroughbred. It was certainly a riding horse, usually small, and sometimes a pacing horse (see *ambulatorius*); often also a horse let out to hire. The Italian *achinea* refers simply to a quiet, ordinary horse.

Haracium (Lat.), *haras*, *haraz* (Fr.): a stud. Though there is unanimity as to the meaning of this word, its derivation has been much contested. (1) In his *Glossarium Mediae et Infimae Latinitatis* (1678) DuCange considered that it must have come from the same root as the French *race* and Italian *razza*, meaning a breed. (2) Others have connected it with the Germanic word for army – OHG *hari*, *heri*, AS *here*, Gothic *harji*. The connection with the Frankish army is attractive, especially since Charlemagne's ancestor, Pepin II (d. 714), was known as 'of Herstal',

Herstal (*Haristallium*, *Heristallium*, or 'the army's stable') being a Frankish palace near Liège. (3) Others, preferring an Arabian origin, have tried to connect *haras* with *faras* (q.v.). They have argued for transmission of that word via either Spain or Byzantium (where it took the form of *pharas*), but have had difficulty in explaining how the initial 'f' changed to 'h'. (4) A more modest derivation is from the Latin *hara*, which originally denoted a pigsty and in Later Latin an enclosure for other beasts, particularly geese. Though this suggests a development like that of the word 'park' (above, pp. 80–81), the gap between pigs and geese on the one hand and horses on the other has still to be bridged. The word's first appearance in England (as *haraz*) is in the Burton Abbey Survey of 1114–15 (above, p. 81).

Hengst (Germ.), *hencgestas* (AS): a confusing term which can denote a stallion, a horse generally or a gelding. It is often impossible to decide which is intended.

Hercator, *hercerius*, *herzorius*: a harrowing horse. Cf. *occatorius*.

Hobilarius: a light horseman, or 'hobelar'. See *hobyn*, and p. 26 above.

Hobyn, *hobi*, *hobin*: a hobby – a small horse or middle-sized pony from Ireland, introduced into England and Scotland towards the end of the thirteenth century. By the fifteenth century the term sometimes denoted a small pacing horse or ambler (see *ambulatorius*).

Hongre (*cheval hongre*) (Fr.): a gelding (q.v.).

Jennet, genet, *ginet* (Fr.), *jineta* (Sp.): a small Spanish horse; also a light horseman.

Jumentum: a mare; this was the meaning from the eighth century at the latest, but in Classical Latin (and as late as the fourth century) it could denote any form of horse or mule. In the Middle Ages it was not the only Latin word for a mare, *equa* being equally common.

Mannus: in Classical Latin a Celtic pony, but it improved its status by degrees, until in the twelfth century the term was used to denote both a horse carrying a litter and a horse ridden by a king in battle (Orderic, iv, 240, vi, 240).

Marescalcia, mariscaltia, mascalcia: horse-medicine. Cf. *mariscalcus*.
Mariscalcus: a marshal, and in the context of this book a horse-doctor. See above, pp. 84–5. His office or position is his 'marshalcy'.
Menescalcia: see *marescalcia*.

Occatorius, occator, equus occarius: a harrowing horse. Cf. *hercator*.

Pacing horse: see *ambulatorius*.
Palefridus: a palfrey, the finest sort of riding horse, as opposed to a warhorse. The word is derived from *paraveredus* (q.v.), but like *caballus* it has gone up in the world.
Paraveredus: a post-horse (second to ninth centuries); subsequently the word developed in Latin as *palefridus* (q.v.), while it also passed into German as *das Pferd*, the ordinary word for horse.
Poledrus: a colt (fifth to ninth centuries).
Pullus: a colt or foal.
Pultrella: a filly.

Runcinus, runcus: In *DB* (1086) the rouncy appears to have been an agricultural workhorse (above, p. 80), but at any rate from the thirteenth century it was an inexpensive (but not cheap) riding horse and the standard mount for an ordinary trooper in the Welsh war of Edward I (see above, p. 67). In these circumstances it is not surprising to find that the root of the word is connected with our generic term 'horse'. O.Fr. *ronci, rous, ross*, Germ. *das Ross* (horse), AS *hors*.

Scutiger, scutarius: a squire or esquire with special duties to the horses. See p. 83.
Silvaticae equae: wild or forest mares, collections of which formed the earliest studs (q.v.).
Sonipes: a horse (a literary and poetical word). Cf. *Cornipes*.
Spada, spado: a spayed horse or gelding (q.v.).
Stalo: a stallion. Cf. *emissarius, waranio*.
Stoned horse: a stallion.
Stottus: a cheap workhorse or plough horse. Cf. *affer*.
Stud: an establishment for the breeding of horses, now usually centred on a stallion (or stallions), but originally signifying a group of mares kept for breeding, the word being derived from the Germ. *die Stute* (mare). The

word thus illustrates the development of breeding from Stage 1 to Stage 3 (above, pp. 38–42).
Summarius: anglicized as 'sumpter', a packhorse.

Thoroughbred: a horse whose pedigree for a given number of generations is in *The General Stud Book*, first published in 1791.
Trottarius, troterius, toletarius: a trotting or ambling horse, but quite a cheap one (the going rate was about 40s. in the middle of the fifteenth century). See *ambulatorius*.

Waranio: a stallion (in Frankish sources of the seventh to ninth centuries). Possibly from Germ. *gären*, to effervesce. Bautier (1976, p. 231) considers *waranio* to be a transposition of the Germ. *wranjo*.

Yard: the virile member of a stallion.

HORSE COLOURS

Bausan, bausant, baucens, baucyn (Fr.), *balzano* (Ital.), *bausond* (ME): white spots on a coloured ground, hence *baybausan, sorbausan, sorelbausan*. Grisone (1550) had qualifications about any horse with white spots on its feet, and considered that if both front feet had these white spots the result would be disastrous.
Bay, *bai* (Fr.) *badius* (Lat.): a chestnut-coloured body (light, bright, dark or brown) with black points (q.v.). It is the black points which distinguish a bay from a chestnut (q.v.).
Bayamblanc (Fr.): bay and white.
Baybaucin (Fr.), *baybausan*: white spots on bay.
Bayclere (Fr.): bright bay.

Chestnut: a horse is called chestnut when not only its body but also its points (q.v.) are of this colour. Cf. bay.

Dappled: marked with roundish (apple-like) spots. Cf. *pommelé*. A dapple grey has dark spots on a grey ground.
Dun: a dull or dingy brown. If almost grey it is called blue dun; if almost brown a golden or yellow dun. Dun horses *may* have black points (q.v.).

Fauvus (Lat.), *fauve* (Fr.), *falbo* (Ital.): tawny (brown with a preponderance of yellow or orange).

Ferrandus (Lat.), *ferraunt* (Fr.): iron grey; also in compounds such as *ferrauntamblanc*, *ferrauntpomyle*, *griselferraunt*.

Grisel (Fr.): grey; hence also *griselferraunt*, *grisliard*, etc.

Lyard, lyart, *liard* (Fr.): very small spots of white on grey, or vice-versa, giving a silver grey appearance. If the grey is predominant over the white, it is called *grisliard*.

Morel (Fr.): shiny black.

Peledargent (Fr.): silver-skin.

Piebald: two different colours, strictly speaking black and white, since the root of the word is the same as in magpie. Cf. skewbald.

Points: the mane, tail and most of the legs.

Pommelé, pomyle (Fr.): marked with round spots as large as an apple.

Roan: a mixed colour with a decided shade of red; often with grey or white spots; hence *ronsorel*.

Skewbald: body marked with large irregular patches of white on any colour except black.

Sor, sorel (Fr.): a bright chestnut colour, reddish brown. As 'sorrel' still used in this sense in America.

Varius (Lat.), *vair* (Fr.): varicoloured or variegated, white or grey with black speckles.

In records horses are often described by a compound word denoting their colour and their previous owner. This is usually clear enough but can lead to confusion if the previous owner's name could be mistaken for a colour. Rousliard is not a 'rosy lyard' but the lyard horse which previously belonged to Rous.

List of Illustrations

Index